Talking
Your Way
to the
TOP

Talking Your Way to the TOP

Business English That WORKS

GRETCHEN S. HIRSCH

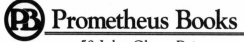 **Prometheus Books**

59 John Glenn Drive
Amherst, New York 14228-2197

Published 2006 by Prometheus Books

Inquiries should be addressed to
Prometheus Books
59 John Glenn Drive
Amherst, New York 14228–2197
VOICE: 716–691–0133, ext. 207
FAX: 716–564–2711
WWW.PROMETHEUSBOOKS.COM

10 09 08 07 06   5 4 3 2 1

Library of Congress Cataloging-in-Publication Data

Hirsch, Gretchen.
    Talking your way to the top : business English that works / by Gretchen S. Hirsch.
        p. cm.
    ISBN-13: 978–1–59102–461–3 (pbk. : alk. paper)
    ISBN-10: 1–59102–461–7 (pbk. : alk. paper)
    1. English language—Business English—Handbooks, manuals, etc. I. Title.

PE1115.H56 2006
808'.042—dc22

2006020199

Printed in the United States of America on acid-free paper

To the memory of my incomparable mother,
Jane Silbernagel,
and to Ruthie Gardner, with deepest gratitude and affection

CONTENTS

PART TWO: SOUNDING SMART AT WORK

PART THREE: TYING IT UP

ACKNOWLEDGMENTS

A special thank you to the following people:

Janet Rosen and Sheree Bykofsky, my agents, for seeing the possibilities.

Linda Regan, my editor, for expanding the possibilities.

My new best friends at Prometheus Books: Ben Keller, Bruce Carle, Jacqueline Cooke, Brian McMahon, and Chris Kramer, for making me and the book look good.

Stew and Lisa Hirsch and Tobey and Scott Huntley, for being the cheering section for this and other projects—and also for being the best kids any mom could have.

The grandboys, Tom, Tyler, Trevor, and Ryan, for providing constant delight and surprise.

My sister and my brother-in-law, Evie and Doug McCord, for lending me their house when I needed quiet.

My brother, Hobie Billingsley, for his amazing generosity.

My cousin, Barbara Brannan, for sharing my love of words and writing.

My writing compatriots Jan Leibovitz Alloy, Susanne Jaffe, Carol Larimer, and Angela Palazzolo, for always encouraging me to go for it—whatever it may be at the moment.

My friends Sue Pidcock, Caroline Planicka, and Sheila Lewis, for lending their assistance long distance, and my local friends, for doing it in person.

The late Roy Patterson, MD, and the late William Hughes, MD, for saving my life, literally.

And, as always, Tony.

INTRODUCTION

In an era characterized by i-messages and e-mail, correct speech still matters. At some point, you have to abandon technology and say something more significant than, "R U OK?" Whether you're the CEO of a conglomerate or a struggling manager, how you speak has an effect on how you're perceived. Grammar gaffes, incorrect word choices, inappropriate language, and inarticulate expression can peg you as ignorant, uneducated, or both.

As the employment market tightens and employers have their pick of qualified applicants, what you say and how you say it may make the difference between being hired and being out on the street again. Ineffective use of language has the power to tie your feet to the bottom rung of the corporate ladder and stall the growth of your career.

In the business world, daily communication toggles between writing and speaking, and reaching the upper echelons requires proficiency in both. For example, when law firm hiring coordinators were asked what abilities they expected law school graduates to bring to their firms, the top two answers were strength in oral communication and competence in written expression. This answer is replicated by human resource directors seeking managers in nearly every industry. When It's Just Business—a San Francisco–based foundation developing a post-university business training curriculum—sought advice from corporate executives and from students themselves, both groups listed courses in writing and speaking as the two most important must-haves. The students knew their skills were lacking, and the executives characterized typical corporate communication as abysmal.

Although weak writing and shoddy speech often go hand in hand, it's somewhat easier to clean up speech than it is to spruce up writing. Many of the issues in writing—homonyms and misspellings, to name just two—don't show up in speech. No one knows if you're saying *fir* or *fur*, *their* or *there*, *who's* or *whose*, or *it's* or *its*, and unless a misspelling changes the way you pronounce a word, no one is the wiser.

Nonetheless, there are still conventions related to the spoken word—and to speak authoritatively requires that you know what they are. In spite of a pressing need for precise spoken communication, schools appear to have abandoned instruction in English usage. Americans mangle their native tongue more—and more creatively—than ever before. Consider the following examples:

- The manager who says, "We *migrated* the computers to the new facility and then *incentivized* our employees to upgrade their skills."
- The respected children's Web site that announces, "*Me* and my pals are going to teach you about shapes."
- The high-priced professional speaker who talks about the damage caused by "racial *epitaphs*."
- The executive assistant who instructs callers to "leave a message for Ms. Jones or *myself*."
- The local reporter who states that a horse has been *drug* under one of the area's dams.

Of course, the proper statements would be:

- "We *moved* the computers to the new facility and *provided incentives* for employees to upgrade their skills."
- "*My pals and I* are going to teach you about shapes."
- The damage caused by "racial *epithets*."
- "Leave a message for Ms. Jones or *me*."
- A horse has been *dragged* under one of the area's dams.

Most people who commit such spoken atrocities have no idea they're speaking incorrectly. They usually have not been taught the basics of oral expression or how to speak effectively, and the result is a hash of nonsensical phrases, weasel words, and jargon that not only sounds bad but also can cost both money and time—two resources business can't afford to waste.

I don't mean to imply that there's only one way to speak. There are many, and the one thing we know about English is that it changes. Slang comes and goes. Styles wax and wane. Pronunciations that were unthinkable fifty years ago are commonplace today. Old words are ushered out, and as new ideas and technologies enter daily life, new words enter the lexicon. That's as it should be.

However, even in a language as forgiving and pliant as English, there are some things that haven't changed. Some constructions and words are still objectively wrong. They aren't matters of style or taste; they aren't subject to fluidity. They're just big, honking mistakes. "Give the letter to *she* and her boss" is wrong. Calling someone a *doctorial* candidate is wrong. Saying that something *gets my dandruff up* is wrong. Referring to the *Klu* Klux Klan is wrong, and *parameterize* is so wrong it isn't even a word, although it sometimes plays one on TV.

How we speak and what we say matters, and not just because some anal-retentive Mrs. Thistlebottom says so. It matters because words are powerful. They are the underpinning of a culture. They provide a common frame of reference and the support on which a society is built. Who controls the words often controls its destiny.

When a dictator overthrows a country, the first thing he does is grab hold of the electronic and print media, because it's essential for him to regulate the conduits through which words travel. And when ethnic conflicts arise, the winners usually try to foist their language on the losers.

Revolutions in which language cannot be controlled are doomed to eventual failure, which is one of the reasons the Internet is so valuable. Although repressive regimes may seize power, the truth is readily available electronically, and the truth travels in words.

The Bible tells us that after the creation of the world the first thing God did was speak. On a somewhat less cosmic scale, you help create your personal destiny in the act of speaking. Research indicates that others form impressions of us in as little as ten to fifteen seconds. Most of us put a great deal of effort into making a positive first impression, but the favorable opinion made by the appropriate clothes, firm handshake, and warm smile can be undone in an instant by hesitant speech and muddled expression.

In many ways, the words you choose reflect who you are; how you express yourself tells others how you think, how knowledgeable you are, how much importance you attach to nuance and precision, and how courteous you are to your listeners. All these things are intangibles, but it's the intangibles that often make the difference in business and personal relationships.

This book began as a collection of mispronunciations, misplaced modifiers, and other miscues I heard. After spending some time in corporate America, I added "business-speak" to the list of unfortunate expressions. As I listened to countless presentations and interviews and sat in on hundreds of meetings, I realized that the problems with oral communication were far more systemic than I had assumed at the beginning, and what I originally envisioned as a short book grew into a larger project with a larger purpose. That purpose is to help others achieve their hearts' desires through the use of language. There's no reason to let a correctable deficit keep you from the success and fulfillment you deserve. Whether you're

a college graduate embarking on your first career, an entre-
preneur wanting to move into the big time, or a corporate
employee looking for the promotion that makes the best use of
your talents and potential, speaking well makes everything
possible—and much easier. Aside from all that, using language
well is a pure pleasure.

Although no single book can cover every situation that
arises, I hope this one will give you some useful information, a
few laughs, and an edge in reaching your most cherished goals.

PART ONE

KEEPING YOUR FOOT OUT OF YOUR MOUTH

THE BASICS

1

WHAT DID YOU SAY?

COMMON MISPRONUNCIATIONS

An occasional mispronunciation is not a capital offense. In fact, those who know the correct pronunciation of a word may be too courteous to tell you if you flub it. However, a string of mispronounced words can make you sound unschooled or lazy, and neither of these is an impression you want to give.

If you've heard a word pronounced several different ways or you're simply unsure of what it should sound like, reach for a dictionary and check out the pronunciation before you use the word. That small act relieves the anxiety of wondering whether you're right, and you immediately speak with more confidence and flair. Most people, even those who appear most knowledgeable, are occasionally surprised to learn they've been pronouncing a word incorrectly, so don't worry about what you've said in the past. Correct it now and continue to apply what you've learned from the dictionary.

As George Bernard Shaw, Winston Churchill, and others have observed, the United States and Great Britain are two countries separated by a common language. For example,

Americans say *PRY-va-cy*, while the British prefer *PRIV-a-cy*. Americans are somewhat divided about *herb*. Some say *urb*; others *hurb*. The British generally prefer the latter. Americans use a *LEV-er*, while the British use a *LEE-ver*. In the United States we try to stay on *SKED-jool*, but our British cousins keep to a *SHED-jool*. Americans who live in the United States are better off using American pronunciations to avoid being considered pompous and patronizing.

Regionalisms and accents are also sometimes a problem. Talking about "feesh"(fish) or "aigs" (eggs) may be perfectly acceptable in Jackson, Ohio, but the words won't be understandable in Fargo, North Dakota, which has its own group of regional pronunciations. There's nothing wrong with regionalisms, and presidents of the United States have demonstrated that you can rise to the top without losing the accent of the South or the Northeast, but business decision-makers often favor Standard American English, which you'll hear if you listen to national newscasts.

The guide to pronunciation I've compiled here is not what you usually find in a Great Big Dictionary. I've tried to keep things simple. How many of us really know what ĕ sounds like?

Many of the words below—*defibrillator* and *sherbet*, for example—are not "business" words; that is, you probably won't use them every day in the office. However, any word you mispronounce in a business setting, from a lunch meeting to a job interview to a presentation to an informal telephone conversation, becomes a business word that can bite you if you don't use it properly.

Listeners who are in a position to hire you, promote you, recommend you, or buy your products may decide not to if persistent mispronunciations make you sound less intelligent than you are. Your inability to speak without a gaggle of errors in pronunciation may make others question your competence in everything. The promotion may go to someone else. You might not land the account. The company may decide not to hire you. Proper speech alone won't get you where you want to go, but impoverished speech will surely hold you back.

BUTCHERED, BUNGLED, AND BLOWN: WORDS YOU SHOULDN'T MISPRONOUNCE

Accessory | *ak-SESS-o-ry*, not *a-SESS-o-ry*. If you remove the *-ory* from this word, what's left? *Access*, not *assess*. Pronounce *access* and then add the rest.

Across | *a-KROSS*, not *a-KROST*. Do you see a *t* anywhere in this word? Didn't think so. So don't add one when you pronounce it.

Aegis | *EE-jis*, not AY-*jis*.

Affadavit | *aff-a-DAY-vit*, not *Aff-a-DAY-vid*. In a moment of madcap caprice, a couple of lawyers might choose to name their son Affa David. But probably not. The last syllable of this word is *it*. Pronounce it with gusto.

All | *all*, not *alls*. There's no gray area here; *alls* is just wrong.

Amphitheater | *AM-fe-thee-a-ter*, not *AMP-i-thee-a-ter*. *Ph* equals *f*.

Analogous | *a-NAL-e-gus*, not *a-NAL-e-jus*.

Antibiotic | *an-ti-bye-OT-ik*, not *an-ti-bee-OT-ik*. Aunt Bee belongs in Mayberry, not in your medicine bottle.

Arctic/Antarctic | *ARK-tik*, not *ART-ik*. Some usage experts may quarrel with this one, and a variety of dictionaries list both. However, many people are adamant about that first hard c. They'll think you're wrong if you omit it, while the people who pronounce the word *ART-ik* probably won't care if you add it. I'd go with the *ARK*, just as Noah did.

Ask

ask, not *ax*. An ax is used to chop down a tree, not to request information.

Asterisk

ASS-te-risk, not *ASS-te-rix* or even *ASS-te-rick*. The last syllable of this word is *risk*. There's an old limerick that will help you recall the correct pronunciation. I don't remember all of it, but the final lines are, "Now wasn't she a silly girl her little ass to risk." You'll never forget again, will you?

Athlete

ATH-lete, not *ATH-a-lete*. This word has only two syllables. Don't give it three. The same goes for the word *athletic*: that word has three syllables, not four.

Arthritis

ar-THRI-tis, not *ar-thur-I-tis*. Arthur may have stiff joints, but this condition wasn't named after him.

Badminton

BAD-min-ton, not *BAD-mit-ten*. When O. J.'s glove didn't fit, the prosecution might have considered it a bad mitten, but badminton is a game played barehanded.

Boutique

boo-TEEK, not *bow-TEEK*. Think Halloween, not Bo Peep.

Business

BIZ-nis, not *BID-nis*, even if you're an auctioneer.

Chamois

For reasons defying explanation, this word is pronounced SHAM-ee.

Chaos	**KAY-oss**, not *chowss*.
Chromosome	*KRO-mo-***sohm**, not *KRO-mo-***sohn**.
Comparable	**KOM**-*per-a-bul*. Put the emphasis on the right syllable. It's not *kom-PARE-a-bul* even though that's what the word means.
Cole Slaw	*KOLE slaw*, not *KO slaw*. Old King Cole loved this dish, so picture His Highness with a big fork.
Congratulations	*kon-gratch-u-LAY-shuns*, not *kon-grad-u-LAY-shuns*, even if you're congratulating a graduate.
Coupon	**KOO**-*pon*, not *KYOO-pon*.
Crayon	**KRAY**-*on*, not *kran*. The only use for *kran* is as a prefix for *berry*.
Debris	*de-***BREE**, not *DEB-ris*. Think of a gangster looking for fine French cheese. He says, "Let's go get de brie." So should you.
Decathlon	*de-KATH-lon*, not *de-KATH-a-lon*. Just as you remove the extra *a* from *athlete*, you also remove it from athletic events. The same rule applies to *biathlon* and *pentathlon*. You'll probably need to know this only during the Olympics, but you'll be proud of yourself when you get it right and the television sports announcers don't.
Defibrillator	*de-FIB-***rill**-*ay-ter*, not *de-FIB-u-lay-ter*. The purpose of a *defibrillator* is to correct fibrillation in the heart, not to keep someone from lying.

Dentist	*DEN-tist*, not *DEN-ist*. Sound the *t* in honor of your teeth, which the dentist works hard to keep healthy. Keep the *t* in *dental*, too, as well as in *rental, gentle, mental*, and any other word in which its omission makes you sound negligent.
Deteriorate	*de-TEER-ee-or-ate*, not *de-TEER-or-ate*. This word has five syllables; pronounce them all.
Deputy	*DEP-u-tee*, not *DEP-i-tee*. Put the right vowel in the middle of the word, and your local sheriff may let you off with a warning.
Dilate	*DI-late*, not *DI-a-late*. Don't dilate this word into three syllables.
Diphtheria	*diff-THEER-i-a*, although because the mispronunciation is so common, most dictionaries now allow *dip-THEER-i-a* as well. However, if you'd like to be on the side of the angels, remember that *ph* equals *f*, even in the middle of a word.
Diphthong	*DIFF-thong*. As with *diphtheria,* dictionaries now also allow *DIP-thong*, which sounds like a skimpy bathing suit. Same issues. Same angels. *Ph* equals *f*—again.
Disastrous	di-*ZAS*-trus, not *di-ZAS-ter-us*. Although clearly *disastrous* is related to *disaster*, this word has only three syllables and no *e*.
Disconcert	*dis-kon-SERT*, not *dis-kon-SERN*.
Doctoral	*DOCK-tor-al*, not *dock-TOR-al*, or even worse, *dock-TOR-i-al*. When you say the

word *doctor*, you emphasize the first syllable. Do the same with this adjective, and remember it has only three syllables.

Doesn't   *DUZZ-ent*, not DUDD-*nt*. Out here at the Lazy S Ranch, we often substitute *d* for *s*, but you shouldn't. Other common words that fall prey to this substitution are *IDD-nt* (*isn't*) and *WUDD-nt* (*wasn't*); all of them sound as if you're just too tired to open your mouth, and that duddn't make a good impression

Duct Tape   *dukt*, not *duck*. Although there is a trademarked product called Duck Tape, unless you are buying this brand, it's *duct* tape. You use it to fix everything but waterfowl.

Ecstatic   *ek-STAT-ik*, not *ess-STAT-ik*. Pronounce the *c* in this word as a *k*, not an *s*.

Electoral   *e-LECK-tor-al*, not *e-leck-TOR-al* or *e-leck-TOR-i-al*. We hold *elections* and *elect* candidates, and the accent is always on the second syllable. Follow the same rule here, no matter how often you hear it mispronounced in the media. Leave out the extra syllable, too.

Environment   *en-VYE-run-ment*, not *en-VYE-er-ment*. Be sure to include the *n* before the *m* in this word.

Epitome   *e-PIT-o-mee*, not *EP-i-tohm*.

Error   *AIR-ur*, not *air*. This word has two syllables; they're both important, so pronounce each of them.

Escape   *ess-CAPE*, not *ex-CAPE*. An ex-cape is
                something Superman donates to charity.

Especially   *e-SPESH-al-ly*, not *ex-PESH-al-ly*. No *k*, no
                x. Pronounce the *s* instead. That's why it's
                there.

Espresso   *es-PRESS-so*, not *ex-PRESS-o*, even if you
                want it really, really fast.

Et cetera   et *SETT-er-a*, not ex *SETT-er-a*. The first syl-
                lable is *et*, pronounced, not surprisingly, *et*.

Familiar   *fa-MILL-yer*, not *fur-MILL-yer*. Animal
                lovers will throw paint on you if pronounce
                the first syllable in this word *fur*.

Fifth   *fifth*, not *fith*. Looking closely, you'll see two
                f's in the word—pronounce them both.

Film   *film*, not *FILL-um*. One syllable only.

Florida   *FLOR-i-da*. This state name has three sylla-
                bles. Don't pronounce it *FLOR-da*.

Formidable   *FORM-id-a-bul*, not *for-MID-a-bul*. The pre-
                ferred pronunciation may be going the way
                of the dodo, but for now it's still the one to
                use.

Genuine   *JENN-u-winn*, not *JENN-u-wine*. You're
                playing tennis with your friend, Jennifer.
                She beats you 6–2, 6–4. You say, "Jen, you
                win," and that's exactly how this word is
                pronounced.

Grievous   *GREE-vus*, not *GREE-vee-us*. This word has
                two syllables, not three. It's typical of a

group of words, such as *mischievous* and *intravenous*, that have been modified by the unnecessary addition of a syllable.

Height

hite, not *hiteth*. Other measurement words, such as *width* and *depth*, end in *th*, but *height* doesn't. Pronounce the final *t* and be done with it.

Heinous

HAY-nuss; not *HIGH-nuss*; not *HINE-ee-us*, which sounds like someone's backside, and certainly not *HEE-nee-us*, which sounds as if you might find it in a zoo.

Hierarchy

HI-er-ark-y, not *HI-ark-y*. A *hierarchy* climbs higher and higher. Make sure the word *higher* is part of your pronunciation of this word.

Huge

Hyooj, not *yooj*. Pronounce the *h* in this word. Do the same when you pronounce *hue*, *human*, *humble*, *humid*, *humor*, and *humongous*.

Hundred

HUNN-dred, not *HUNN-durd* or *HUNN-erd*. It's dreadful if you don't say *hundred* correctly.

Hyperbole

hy-PER-ba-lee, not *HY-per-bowl*. The second pronunciation sounds like the Big Game on steroids—and surely there are no steroids in sports.

Hypnotize

HIPP-no-tize, not *HIPP-mo-tize*. Most people pronounce *hypnosis* correctly, but many stumble over the verb form. Remember that the second syllable is *no*, as in, "No, I can't be hypnotized."

Illinois

ill-an-OY, not *ill-an-OYZ*. It's only one state, after all, so don't make it plural.

Incomparable

in-KOM-per-a-bul. Same rule as *comparable*.

Insurance

in-SURE-ance, not IN-sure-ance. You want to be *sure* you have insurance, so emphasize that fact and that syllable.

Integral

IN-te-gral or even *in-TEG-ral*, but not *IN-tri-gel*. Put the *r* in the right place, which is the third syllable, not the second. *Integral* and *integrate* have the same root, and you don't say *intregate*, do you?

Intravenous

in-tra-VEE-nuss, not *in-tra-VEE-ni-us*. Four syllables only. Don't pronounce what isn't there. *Venous* means "pertaining to veins" and it doesn't need an additional *i*.

Iran/Iraq

There is no *eye* sound in either of these words. It's *i-RAHN* and *i-RAHK*, or *i-RAN* and *i-RAK*, but it's not correct to say *eye-RAN* or *eye-RAK* any more than it's correct to say *eye-TAL-i-an*.

Jaguar

In the United States, it's *JAG-wahr*, not *JAG-wire*, although hot-wiring a Jag sounds like a lot of fun. In Great Britain, it's pronounced *JAG-yu-wahr*, and since the car originated in England, even some American enthusiasts maintain that pronunciation.

Jewelry

JOO-el-ree, not *JOO-le-ree*. The most important part of this word is not *joo*, but *jewel*. Pronounce *jewel* fully before you add the *ree*.

Ku Klux Klan	***Koo** Klux Klan*, not *Klu Klux Klan*. The Klan doesn't have a clue, so don't give them one.
Lackadaisical	***lack**-a-DAY-zi-kal*, not *lax-i-DAY-zi-kal*. Although this word suggests a certain laxity of vigor, the first syllable is *lack*, not *lax*.
Lambaste	*lam-**BASTE***, not *lam-BAST*. You're grilling a leg of lamb. You occasionally coat it with liquid to keep it moist. That liquid is lamb baste, and so is this word.
Larynx	*LAIR-**inks***, not *LAR-nix*. Your larynx is important; don't nix it.
Line	*line*, not *LYE-un*. If you want a lion, go to the zoo.
Length/Strength	*Leng**k**th or streng**k**th*, not *lenth* or *strenth*. The *g* makes a *k* sound. Unlike *height*, these words end in *th*.
Library	*LYE-**brer**-y*, not *LYE-berr-y*. There's a blueberry, a raspberry, and a strawberry, but there's no lyeberry. Think of Br'er Rabbit and pronounce both *r*'s.
Masonry	*MAY-son-**ry***, not *MAY-son-air-y*. A carpenter does carpentry. A cabinet maker does cabinetry. We don't call those crafts carpentary or cabinetary, and masons don't do masonary, either. Take out the extra syllable to pronounce it properly.
Mayonnaise	***may**-o-NAYZ*. Women often use this condiment, so don't pronounce it *MAN-ayz*.

Mirror	*MEER-**ur***, not MEER. This word has two syllables and three *r*'s. Pronounce both syllables and at least two *r*'s. If you say *Mir*, one can only assume you're talking about the Russian space station.
Mischievous	*MISS-che-vuss*, not *mis-CHEE-vee-us*. *Mischievous* grows out of the word *mischief*, not *mischeeve*, and it has only three syllables, not four.
Mower	*MOH-**wer***, not *more*. Surely your mouth can handle two syllables. Just as with *error* and *mirror*, finish these words by using all the syllables.
-mycin	*-mycin* is a suffix applied to many pharmaceuticals. *-mycin* has only two syllables and is pronounced *MY-sin* (just as if you were confessing it proudly), not *MY-a-sin*.
Nine	***nine***, not *NY-un*.
Nuclear	*NOO-**klee**-er*, not *NOO-kyoo-ler*. The center of an atom is the *nucleus,* not the *nuculus,* and the adjective referring to the nucleus is *nuclear*.
Nuptial	*NUPP-**shul***, not *NUPP-chew-al*. Two syllables, not three.
Obvious	*OBB-vee-us*, not *ODD-vee-us*. It's odd that this pronunciation is so common because it's so wrong.
Often	*OFF-**en***, not *OFF-ten*. If you make a subtraction mistake, the answer might be off ten, but in this word the *t* is silent.

Ophthalmologist	The MD or DO who treats conditions of the eye is an *ahff-thal-MOLL-o-jist*, not an *op-thal-MOLL-o-jist*. The graduate of a school of optometry (an OD) is an *op-TOMM-e-trist*, and that's what causes the confusion between the two words. See that *ph* in the first syllable? It equals *f*, once again.
Ostensibly	*aw-STENN-sib-lee*, not *aw-STENN-sive-lee*. Look at the third syllable. It's sib (like a brother or sister), not sieve.
Oxymoron	*ock-see-MOR-on*, not *ock-SIM-ir-on*. If you put the *moron* in this word, then you won't sound like one.
Pastoral	*PAS-tor-al*, not *pas-TOR-al* or *pas-TOR-i-al*. When we say *pastor*, we accent the first syllable. Do the same thing here and don't add an extra syllable.
Percolate	*PURR-ko-late*, nor *PURR-kyoo-late*. Think of the first two letters of *coffee*, which is percolated; that'll get you there.
Peripheral	*Per-IFF-er-ul*, not *per-IF-ree-ul*. Don't reverse the letters in the third syllable.
Perseverance	*Per-se-VEER-ance*, not *pers-er-VEER-ance*. Skip the extra *r*.
Perspiration	*pers-pi-RAY-shun*, not *press-pir-RAY-shun*. Most people don't say *prespire*, so let's not mispronounce this one, either.
Plenitude	*PLENN-i-tude*, not *PLENN-ti-tude*. Although having a *plenitude* of something means you have plenty, there's only one *t* in this word.

Plethora   ***PLETH-o-ra***, not *ple-THOR-a*. This is one of those accent-on-the-wrong-syllable traps that can snare even the most careful speaker.

Porsche   *POR-**sha***, not *porsh*. I've heard it said that the correct pronunciation is the mark of a show-off, but in fact, it's simply a mark of respect. Porsche is the German family name of the manufacturer, and it should be pronounced the way the family pronounces it. If your family name is *Smythe*, do you want someone pronouncing it *Smith* just because he's worried about sounding pretentious?

Posthumous   ***POS-che-muss***, not *post-HYOO-muss*, which sounds like something you put on after you add fertilizer.

Potable   ***POH-ta-bul***, not *POTT-a-bul*. Although in some countries, water is carried in pots, much of the water transported that way might not be *potable*, which means "fit for drinking."

Precedence   ***PRESS-i-dence***, not *pre-SEED-ence*. Although *precedence* is related to the word *precede*, the pronunciation is completely different.

Preferable   ***PREFF-er-a-bul***, not *per-FERR-a-bul*. Although this word is related to *prefer*, it follows the same rule as *preference*, with the accent on the first syllable.

Prescription   ***pre-SCRIPP-shun***, not *per-SCRIPP-shun*. Many people mispronounce a variety of words beginning with *pre* or *per*; if you're not sure what the prefix is, look it up.

Prerogative — *pre-ROGG-a-tiv*, not *per-ROGG-a-tiv*.

Probably — *PROBB-a-blee*. Don't pronounce it *PROBB-lee*, or worse, *PROLL-lee*. Sound all three syllables.

Pronunciation — *pro-nun-see-AY-shun*, not *pro-noun-si-AY-shun*. Isn't it ironic that one of the most commonly mispronounced words is pronunciation? Look at the word. See the little *nun* in the second syllable? That's Sister Mary Uptight, and she'll rap your knuckles with a ruler if you pronounce the word *pronunciation* incorrectly.

Proviso — *pro-VYE-zo*, not *pro-VEE-zo*.

Realtor — *REEL-tor*, not *REE-la-ter*. *Realt*ors sell *real* estate. Say *real*, and then say *tor*. That's it.

Radiator — *RAY-dee-ay-ter*, not RADD-*ee-ay-ter*. This device, which is not radical, radiates heat.

Recognize — *RECK-og-nize*, not *RECK-a-nize*. Be sure to recognize that there's a *g* in this word—and it's not silent.

Refrigerator — *re-FRIJ-er-ay-ter*, not *FRIJ-er-ay-ter*. To avoid this word altogether, you can call it a *fridge*, or if you want to show everyone you're really old, an *icebox*.

Rigamarole (or rigmarole) — *RIG-a-ma-roll*, not *RIG-a-ma-roe*. This word means a rambling and incoherent statement and has nothing to do with the eggs of the rigama fish.

Reprise	*re-PREEZ*, not *re-PRIZE*. There are no prizes for doing something over.
Respite	***RESS-pit***, not *re-SPITE*. A respite is like a pit stop when life gets going too fast.
Salmon	***SAM-un***, not *SAL-mun*. The *l* is not pronounced.
Sandwich	***SAND-witch***. Not *SAN-witch*. Not *SAM-witch*, and not *SANG-witch*, either. Think of the food you eat at the beach. It might be full of sand—just like this word.
Sherbet	*SHUR-**bit***, not *SHUR-bert*. "Sure, Bert," is what Ernie says to his pal, but it's not the name of this icy dessert. Think of it as a sure bet on a hot afternoon, and you'll be close to the correct pronunciation.
So	*so*, not *sohz*. If you're speaking in dialect, you can get by with *sohz*, I suppose, but it's never correct elsewhere.
Spurious	*SPYOOR-ee-us*, not *SPUR-ee-us*.
Succinct	*suck-SINGKT*, not *suh-SINGKT*. Suck it up and pronounce the entire first syllable.
Supremacist	*suh-PREMM-**a**-sist*, not *suh-PREMM-ist*. This word has four syllables, not three.
Suppose	***suh**-POHZ*. Not *spohz*. Sound both syllables.

Supposedly

suh-POHZ-ed-lee, not suh-POHZ-ub-lee. This "ly" form is based on the word *supposed* (pronounced *suh-POHZ-ed*). There is no word *suh-POHZ-ub*, so the reason for this mispronunciation is a mystery.

Terrorism

TAIR-ur-izm, not *TAIR-izm*. It's sad that we've come to know this word so intimately, but since it's now part of our daily lexicon, we have to pronounce it properly. It has four syllables, not three. Don't say *TAIR-ist*, either. It's *TAIR-ur-ist*. These people aren't ripping up pieces of paper; they're spreading terror.

Twenty

TWENN-tee, not *TWENN-ee*. Most people get all the *-ty* numbers right: *thirty, forty, fifty*, but for some reason, *twenty* escapes them. Pronounce that second *t* or you sound almost too lethargic to breathe.

Twice

TWICE, not *TWICET*. There's only one *t* in this word and it's at the beginning. (The same rule applies to *Once* and *Oncet*.)

Valentine

VAL-en-tine, not *VAL-en-time*. Saint Valentine was a person, and he probably didn't wear a watch.

Veterinarian

vet-ur-in-AIR-ee-un, not *vet-in-AIR-ee-un*. This work has six syllables—all six should be pronounced. Or just say *vet*.

Vice versa

VICE vur-sa, not *VICE-a vur-sa*. It seems logical that this phrase would have four syllables, but it has only three.

W	*DUBB-**ul-yoo***, not *DUBB-ya* or *DUBB-yoo*, no matter what the press calls Bush 43.
Wash	*wash*. There is no *r* in the word *wash*. Avoid *warsh* and *Warshington*, both the state and the nation's capital.
Wheelbarrow	*Hweel-bair-oh*. Be sure to notice that this word is not *wheelbarrel*. Barrows and barrels are two different types of containers, and only a barrow has wheels.
Wholesale	*HOLE-sayl*, not *HO-sayl*. If you drop the *l* it sounds as if you're auctioning off ladies of the evening.
Wimbledon	*WIMM-bul-**dun***, not *WIMM-bul-ton*.
Zealous	*ZELL-us*, not *zee-lus*. Although this word is derived from the noun *zeal*, when it becomes an adjective, the pronunciation of the first syllable changes.
Zoology	*zoh-OLL-o-jee*. There's no zoo in zoology.

If you've been pronouncing any of the above words incorrectly, practice the new pronunciations until they become more familiar. This will get you in the mood for the next step in polishing your oral prose.

2

THE WRONG WORD AT THE WRONG TIME

You're cruising along as you give a speech before a professional organization. Your facts are compelling and your visuals eye-catching. You look like a leader; you sound like an authority—and then you say you'll illustrate your point with a few *antidotes*. Your audience lapses into nudge-nudge, wink-wink mode; you've lost at least a portion of your credibility, just when you need it most.

Word pairs that sound similar but have different meanings have confused many a speaker. Is it *adverse* or *averse*? *Cache* or *cachet*? *Enormous* or *enormity*? Then there are words that have different meanings but are sometimes used interchangeably and often incorrectly. Is it *advise* or *inform*? *Disinterested* or *uninterested*? *Jail* or *prison*? *Lectern* or *podium*? Because no one knows every word in the dictionary, everyone makes an occasional mistake, but when you consistently make the wrong choice, you run the risk of sounding ill-prepared and incompetent. You can eliminate that perception by knowing and using the right word in the right context.

Here are some problematic pairs and sneaky singletons to look out for:

MATCHED SETS

Note: n indicates noun; v, verb; pron, pronoun; and adj, adjective.

Abrogate/   *Abrogate* means "cancel or repeal." *Arro-*
Arrogate   *gate* means "claim something without right."

Example: Congress abrogated the trade agreement.

Example: Dan arrogated all the strategic decisions to himself instead of seeking consensus.

Administer/   An administrator *administers*; he need not
Administrate   *administrate.* Although some dictionaries accept *administrate*, they do so with the proviso that *administer* is preferred.

Adverse/Averse   *Adverse* means "unfavorable." *Averse* means "unwilling." They are both adjectives and they look alike, but they have vastly different meanings. Don't say, "I'm not adverse to . . ."

Example: We weren't expecting such an adverse result.

Example: She isn't averse to conducting the experiment again.

Advice/Advise/   *Advice* means "an opinion or piece of infor-
Inform   mation." *Advise* means "offer advice"; *inform* means "offer information."

Example: Let me offer you some advice on your budgeting process.

Example: This letter is to inform you that you're eligible for a new banking product. As your personal banker, I advise you to set up your account as quickly as possible.

Affect/Effect   Affect, which means "influence or change," is almost always a verb. The only time it is used as a noun is when it describes someone's face or demeanor. *Effect*, which means "change produced by an action," is almost always a noun. The only time it is used as a verb is when it means "bring about a purpose."

Example: Stan's resignation affected (v) the entire organization.

Example: Her mental illness caused her to have a very flat affect [n; pronounced *AFF-eckt*].

Example: Liza's enthusiasm almost always has a positive effect [n] on others.

Example: The bonuses effected [v] a huge change in morale.

Aggravate/   *Aggravate* means "make worse." *Annoy*
Annoy   means "bother."

Example: Joel's ridiculous excuse for missing the meeting aggravated the situation.

Example: Billy annoyed his assistant every day.

Almost/Most   *Almost* means "nearly." *Most* means "the greatest number."

Example: Almost the entire office staff resigned.

Example: Most of them could no longer tolerate Marcy's attitude.

Alternate/   *Alternate* (v; pronounced *ALL-tur-nayt*)
Alternative   means "pass from one state to another by turns." *Alternate* (n; pronounced *ALL-tur-nit*) means "deputy or substitute." *Alternative* means "one of two or more exclusive possibilities."

Example: The board alternated between tabling and disapproving the motion.

Example: Since Henry couldn't attend the conference, we sent Fritz as his alternate.

Example: John wrote alternative endings for his report on the new public relations program.

Alumna/   *Alumna* means "female graduate." *Alumnus*
Alumnus   is "male graduate." The plural of *alumna* is *alumnae* (pronounced *a-LUMM-nee*), and the plural of *alumnus* is *alumni* (*a-LUMM-nye*). When the group of graduates includes both males and females, they are referred to as *alumni*. It's a guy thing.

Ambiguous/   *Ambiguous* means "having more than one
Ambivalent   possible meaning." *Ambivalent* means "having conflicting feelings."

Example: This ruling is so ambiguous I can't make heads or tails of it.

Example: We're ambivalent about relocating the company. There's a great workforce here, but the tax situation is better there.

Anecdote/   *Anecdote* means "short, illustrative story."
Antidote   *Anecdotal* is the adjective form of *anecdote*. *Antidote* means "substance that counteracts a poison."

Example: Sheila told an interesting anecdote to illustrate her point.

Example: Her conclusions were based solely on anecdotal evidence.

Example: After the snake bit him, we rushed Barney to the hospital for the antidote.

Anxious/Eager   *Anxious* means "full of anxiety." *Eager* means "impatiently expectant."

Example: Joan was anxious about meeting the vice president, but he was eager to see if her consulting skills were as sharp as he had heard.

Appraise/   *Appraise* means "set a value on." *Apprise*
Apprise   means "inform."

Example: We'll be happy to appraise your real estate assets, and we'll apprise you of their value when we've finished our work.

As/Like   *Like* and *as* are used to make comparisons. *Like* is a preposition; use it when the things you are comparing are nouns or pronouns. *As* is a conjunction; use it to join clauses that contain verbs.

Example: I [pron] felt like a fool [n] when I discovered my mistake.

Example: I felt [v] as if I should apologize [v].

Assure/Ensure/   *Assure* means "give confidence or con-
Insure   vince." *Ensure* means "make certain or
                  guarantee." *Insure* means "buy or issue
                  insurance for."

Example: We all tried to assure Vicki that her presentation would be great.

Example: I want to ensure delivery of the package by Saturday.

Example: The company will insure your new capital equipment purchase.

Astigmatism/   *Astigmatism* is a type of defect of the eye
A stigma   that causes poor focus. Although it is pro-
                  nounced as if it were two words—"a stigma-
                  tism"—it's really only one. A *stigma* is a mark
                  of shame or disgrace. Note that it's two words.

Example: I have to wear special lenses to counteract my severe astigmatism.

Example: In this company, there's a stigma about making even the smallest error.

As to whether/   Just say *whether*. The other choices are
Whether/   redundant.
Whether or not

Example: We wondered whether the meeting had been rescheduled.

Average/Mean/ Median	*Average* and *mean* have the same meaning, which is "number gained by adding all the units in a group and dividing by the number of units." *Median* means "the middle value when a list of values is arranged from largest to smallest."

Example: The average contribution to Al's campaign was $1,761, but the median was only $250. One big donation skewed the mean.

Bacteria/ Bacterium	*Bacteria* is the plural of *bacterium*. If you mean one germ, say *bacterium*. Lots of them? *Bacteria*.

Example: The outbreak was caused by a bacterium.

Example: The hotel kitchen was a hotbed of bacteria.

Bad/Badly	If you *feel badly*, the listener might infer that there's something wrong with your sense of touch. The word *feel* requires an adjective, not an adverb. You say *I feel happy* (not happily) or *I feel sad* (not sadly), so I feel bad is the correct choice.

Example: Helen felt so bad that she'd insulted Kim.

Beside/Besides	*Beside* means "next to." *Besides* means "in addition to."

Example: All the younger women angled for a seat beside Ryan.

Example: Who besides Anna is going to the meeting?

Bring/Take	*Bring* means "convey toward the speaker." *Take* means "convey away from the speaker."

Example: Please bring the salad to the office party and take the leftovers home with you.

Burglary/
Robbery
Burglary means "illegally entering a building with intent to steal." *Robbery* means "taking something of value by force."

Example: The burglary occurred just minutes after everyone had left the office.

Example: John was robbed in the lobby of the convention center.

By accident/
On accident
The phrase *on accident* has become popular in various regions of the country, but *by accident* is preferred. A few experts think that those who say *on accident* use the phrase to mean the opposite of *on purpose.*

Example: Freddy found the formula almost by accident.

Example: Larry suppressed the irregularities in the books on purpose.

Cache/Cachet
Cache (pronounced *cash*) means "hidden valuables or treasure." It also means "a portion of a computer where frequently accessed data can be stored for rapid retrieval." *Cachet* (pronounced *ka-SHAY*) means "prestige."

Example: The dictator kept a cache of diamonds in the palace in case he had to flee the country.

Example: Emptying your cache might speed up your computer.

Example: Ron felt there was a certain cachet in belonging to the country club.

Calvary/Cavalry   *Calvary* is the place where Jesus was crucified. *Cavalry* means "troops that fight on horseback or in armored vehicles."

Example: There were Roman soldiers on Calvary.

Example: The consultants came in like the cavalry riding to the rescue of the company.

Can/May   *Can* means "has the ability and knowledge to do something." *May* means "has permission to do something."

Example: Can you fix your own computer?

Example: May I ride with you to the meeting?

Caramel/Carmel   *Caramel* (pronounced *CAIR-a-mell*) means "melted sugar used for coloring or flavoring or foods that feature such flavoring." *(Mount) Carmel* (pronounced *CAR-mel*) is a ridge of land in Israel. Of course, *Carmel* (pronounced *car-MELL*) is a town in California. It's preferable to use *caramel* when referring to cooking, except in the case of "carmel corn." Everybody says that and nobody cares.

Example: The caterer charged a fortune for the chocolate caramels in our hospitality suite.

Censor/Censure   *Censor* means "remove or ban material deemed to be offensive or harmful." *Censure* means "rebuke."

Example: The CFO censored portions of the report before it was released to the board.

Example: The board censured both the CEO and CFO for omitting the critical information.

Chalice/Challis   *Chalice* means "cup or goblet." *Challis* (pronounced *SHAL-ee*) is a type of a printed fabric.

Example: The bride and groom drank out of a chalice at their wedding ceremony.

Example: Jody wore her challis skirt and velvet jacket to the wedding.

Click/Clique   *Click* means "short, sharp sound." *Clique* (pronounced *kleek*) means "small, exclusive group."

Example: The door closed with a click.

Example: Tom wouldn't have anything to do with the snobbish clique from headquarters.

Climactic/   *Climactic* means "pertaining to a climax."
Climatic   *Climatic* means "pertaining to climate."

Example: Stew missed the climactic moment of the argument between the two assistants.

Example: Climatic conditions will dictate whether our opening event will include outdoor activities.

Comment/   Although some dictionaries (those that
Commentate   admit every word ever spoken, correct or

incorrect) allow *commentate*, it's not pre-ferred, and those who use it sound full of themselves. A commentator comments or provides commentary.

Example: Trevor offered perceptive comments about the stock's performance.

Complected/
Complexion/
Complexioned

Complected is very substandard usage. Even some of the most lax dictionaries don't recognize it. Remove it from your vocabulary.

Example: The thief had a fair complexion and bright red hair.

Example: My daughter is dark complexioned.

Complement/
Compliment

Complement means "complete or supplement." *Compliment* means "praise." The second syllable makes a big difference.

Example: The brochure complements the annual report beautifully. You deserve a compliment for your work on it.

Compose/
Comprise

Compose means "make up or constitute something else." *Comprise* means "include." Do not say *is comprised of*.

Example: The division comprises [includes] seven departments.

Example: The division is composed [made up] of seven departments.

Confidant/
Confident

A *confidant* is a person in whom one feels free to confide. The female form of the word is *confidante*. *Confident* means "sure of oneself."

Example: Karen told only her closest confidantes about the changes she'd make after she received her promotion.

Example: Tony is the most confident salesperson in the company.

Conscience/ Conscious

Conscience means "one's internal sense of morality or ethics." *Conscious* means "being aware of one's environment."

Example: Candy wanted to keep the money she found in the empty cubicle, but her conscience wouldn't let her.

Example: We worked all night, and I was so tired I was barely conscious.

Consummate/ Consummate

Consummate (v) means "accomplish or complete," and it's pronounced *KONN-su-mayt*. A specialized meaning is to complete by sexual intercourse, that is, to consummate a marriage. That meaning is pronounced the same way. *Consummate* (adj) means "very skilled," and it's pronounced *konn-SUM-mit or KONN-sum-it*.

Example: We'll consummate the deal Monday.

Example: Fred and Ethel consummated their marriage, so it was difficult for them to get an annulment.

Example: John is a consummate negotiator.

Continual/ Continuous	*Continual* means "at intervals." *Continuous* means "without a break."

Example: The copier continually broke down.

Example: The siren blared continuously for three minutes.

Conversant/ Conversate/ Converse	*Conversant* means "having knowledge of." *Conversate* is a corruption of the word *converse*, which means "engage in conversation or discussion." *Conversate* is always incorrect, so don't use it.

Example: Are you conversant with all aspects of the manufacturing process?

Example: Theo and Don conversed freely about many topics.

Convince/ Persuade	*Convince* means "cause belief." *Persuade* means "cause action."

Example: We all convinced José that our viewpoint was right, and then we persuaded him to write the memo presenting our position.

Core/Corps/ Corpse	*Core* (pronounced *korr*) means the central part of something. *Corps* (pronounced *korr*) means a military force. *Corpse* (pronounced *korps*) means a lifeless body.

Example: Honesty is at the core of our business philosophy.

Example: Before he joined the company, Andre was in the Marine Corps.

Example: The police discovered the corpse behind the factory.

Cornet/Coronet   A *cornet* is a type of brass instrument similar to a trumpet. *Coronet* means "small crown."

Example: John's boss also plays the cornet in a jazz band.

Example: The senior partner's wife is so flashy; she wore a diamond coronet to the firm's holiday dinner.

Credible/
Creditable/
Credulous
Credible means "worthy of belief." *Creditable* means "worthy of credit." *Credulous* means "gullible."

Example: Gus is a very credible source. He always has his facts straight.

Example: Leigh did a creditable job of teaching the keyboarding course.

Example: Gussie is so credulous she'll believe anything you tell her.

Creek/Crick   *Creek* means "small body of running water." *Crick* means "painful cramp."

Example: The creek dried up during the long, hot summer.

Example: I have such a crick in my neck I can't turn my head.

Criteria/
Criterion
Criteria is the plural of *criterion*. Do not use these words interchangeably.

Example: One criterion for acceptance into the program is completion of a business-related project.

Example: These criteria are difficult to fulfill.

Currently/ Presently

Currently means "now." *Presently* means "soon."

Example: The boss is currently in a meeting.

Example: He'll be coming to your office presently.

Dander/ Dandruff

Dander means "spirit or temper." It can also mean "dry skin shed by animals." Although dander is similar to dandruff in humans, the common misuse has to do with the first meaning. *Dandruff* means "flaky skin from the scalp."

Example: Bobbie's comments really got my dander up.

Example: Jake is violently allergic to cat dander.

Example: Before I began my interview, I checked the shoulders of my jacket to see if I had any dandruff.

Defuse/Diffuse

Defuse means "reduce tension" or "disarm a bomb." *Diffuse* means "spread out."

Example: Adam was able to defuse the friction between the CEO and the CFO.

Example: The rain diffused the pollen, and everyone stopped sneezing.

Discomfit/
Discomfort

Discomfit (v) means "make uneasy or embarrass." *Discomfort* (n) means "mental or bodily distress that negatively affects one's level of comfort."

Example: Howard was discomfited when the sales figures came out. His division was at the bottom of the list.

Example: Howard was in great discomfort from his tennis injury.

Disillusion/
Dissolution

Disillusion means "free from illusion." *Dissolution* means "disintegration or state of being dissolved."

Example: The firm's three principals quickly became disillusioned with one another, so they sought dissolution of their two-month partnership.

Disinterested/
Uninterested

Disinterested means "unbiased or neutral." *Uninterested* means "indifferent or showing no interest or sympathy."

Example: He was a good mediator because he was disinterested in the outcome.

Example: She was uninterested in her coworkers' opinions.

Distinct/
Distinctive

Distinct means "perceptible or clear." It can also mean "different in kind." *Distinctive* means "having a quality that sets a thing apart from other things."

Example: Max speaks quickly but distinctly.

Example: Rudy's language in the office is distinct from the way he speaks elsewhere.

Example: You can always find Sarah in a crowd because she wears such distinctive jackets.

Drag /Dragged/ Drug

Drag (v) means means "haul or tug." The past tense is *dragged*, not *drug*. *Drug* (n) means "medication," which can include narcotics. *Drug* also can mean an "illegal substance, such as hallucinogens or meth-amphetamine, used to alter consciousness."

Example: We dragged the copier into the room that hadn't been flooded.

Example: Aspirin is truly a miracle drug.

Drowned/ Drownded

The present tense of this word is *drown*. If the event happened in the past, the correct usage is *drowned*. There is no such word as *drownded*.

Example: Hector was drowned in paperwork.

-een/-ing

Thousands of English words end in *-ing*, and thousands of people pronounce *ing* as if it were spelled *een*: *go-een, leav-een, read-een, morn-een*. Other speakers drop the *g*, as in *goin', comin',* or *speakin'*. If you want to sound smart, you'll concentrate on putting the *-ing* back where it belongs and keeping the *g as well*.

Effete/ Effeminate

Effete means "worn out or robbed of vitality." *Effeminate* means "possessing feminine qualities."

Example: The new sales concept was effete.

Example: Harry is the most effeminate man I know.

Electric/ Electricity	*Electric* (adj) means "of or operated by electricity." *Electricity* (n) means "current used as a source of power." It is not correct to say, "We're having our electric installed today," because as an adjective, *electric* has to have a word to modify.

Example: We have an electric stove in the office kitchenette.

Example: We're having our electricity [or electric service] installed today.

Emigrate/ Immigrate	*Emigrate* means "leave one's country of origin to live in another." *Immigrate* means "settle in a new country."

Example: The family emigrated from [left] Germany in 1834.

Example: They immigrated [came] to Canada.

Eminent/ Imminent	*Eminent* means "famous or distinguished." *Imminent* means "occurring soon."

Example: The eminent CEO explained his theories about market fluctuations.

Example: The executives' indictments are imminent.

Energize/ Enervate	*Energize* means "impart energy to." *Enervate* means "exhaust."

Example: A new project always energizes Tyler, but when the work is done, he's enervated.

Enormity/
Enormous

Enormity implies evil. It has nothing to do with size. *Enormous* describes size.

Example: The enormity of the CFO's malfeasance has yet to be determined.

Example: The new plant is enormous, covering twelve city blocks.

Enthused/
Enthusiastic

Both *enthused* and *enthusiastic* mean "full of excitement," but in careful speech, *enthusiastic* is preferred. In some settings, you may be able to get by with *enthused*, but many listeners cringe at the word. Why take the chance?

Example: Pedro was enthusiastic about his transfer to the office in Madrid.

Entomology/
Etymology

Entomology is the study of insects. *Etymology* is the study of word origins. An entomologist can identify a cockroach. An etymologist can tell you why it's called a cockroach.

Example: Can you tell me the etymology of the word *etymology*?

Example: George is an entomologist who specializes in bees and wasps.

Epitaph/Epithet

Epitaph means "inscription on a tombstone." An *epithet* is a word, often abusive, used in place of or with a name to characterize something.

Example: The musician's epitaph was *One More Time*.

Example: We do not allow racial or ethnic epithets on our premises.

Equally as   Do not use these two words together. Choose one or the other.

Example: He was as tall as Scott.

Example: He and Scott were equally tall.

Explicit/   *Explicit* means "clearly stated." *Implicit*
Implicit   means "understood, but unspoken."

Example: The editor was explicit about the style she preferred.

Example: Respect for her employees is implicit in Jane's management style.

Famous/   *Famous* means "well known to many
Infamous   people." *Infamous* means "having a bad reputation"; it's about being famous for the wrong reasons.

Example: Riley is famous for his inventions.

Example: Alex is infamous for trying to steal others' ideas.

Farther/Further   *Farther* refers to distance. *Further* refers to time or degree.

Example: How much farther is it to Albuquerque?

Example: We will look further into the reasons the electric grid failed.

Ferment/
Foment

Ferment means "state of seething excitement or agitation." *Foment* means "stir up or stimulate."

Example: Bill fomented an employee rebellion that kept the whole office in ferment for weeks.

Fever/
Temperature

Fever means "abnormally high body temperature." *Temperature* means "intensity of heat or cold." Everyone has a temperature—room temperature if you happen to be dead—but not everyone has a fever. And by the way, temperature has four syllables: pronounce it *TEMM-pur-a-chur*, not *TEMM-pa-chur*.

Example: John had a high fever, so he couldn't attend the team-building weekend.

Example: The temperature in the room was below 40 degrees.

Fewer/Less

Fewer refers to countable, individual items. *Less* is used with uncountable bulk quantities. However, everybody says *one less thing to worry about*, and that's okay.

Example: The "Healthy Selection" dinners at our new restaurant contain less fat and fewer calories.

Figuratively/
Literally

Figuratively means "symbolically." *Literally* means "actually."

Example: He said he was so hungry he could eat a horse—figuratively, of course.

Example: I was literally knocked out when the door hit me in the head.

Flaunt/Flout   *Flaunt* means "display or show off." *Flout* means "disregard scornfully."

Example: She flaunted her award until everyone was sick of it—and her.

Example: He flouted all the policies and procedures instead of following them.

Florid/Livid/ Sanguine   Both *florid* and *sanguine* mean "flushed, ruddy, or rosy." *Livid* means "pale or ashen." It can also mean "angry," but it doesn't mean "red-faced with fury."

Example: When Frank heard about the dip in the stock price, his face became livid.

Example: Frank's complexion is naturally florid, so sometimes he looks angry when he isn't.

Flounder/ Founder   *Flounder* means "thrash about." *Founder* means "sink."

Example: When Bettina was thrown into the lake at the company picnic, she floundered for a minute before we realized she couldn't swim.

Example: The company is foundering in a sea of red ink.

Fortunate/
Fortuitous

Fortunate means "having good fortune." *Fortuitous* means "happening by chance." Both good and bad events can be fortuitous, but a fortunate event is always happy.

Example: It was fortunate that Joan discovered the accounting errors before the annual report went to press.

Example: Florence's accident was fortuitous. The safety straps holding the piano broke just as she was walking under it.

Full/Fulsome

Full means "at capacity." *Fulsome* means "cloying or excessive."

Example: The auditorium was full, so we had to schedule an additional meeting.

Example: Her fulsome praise didn't ring true.

Go/Say

Teenagers use *go* in the place of *say* all the time ("So I go, 'You're kidding,' and he goes, 'No way.'") Adults shouldn't. It sounds, like, stupid. See *like/say*.

Good/Well

Do not use *good* to modify a verb—for example, *I played* (or *performed* or *ate*) *good*—unless of course, you are a professional athlete, which also entitles you to say *you know* forty-three times in a two-minute interview. *Well* is the adverb, so please say, "He did well."

Graduate/
Graduate from

Graduate from is the correct usage. One who graduates from school is a graduate. It's also correct to say that someone graduated first (or last or anywhere in between) in his class. But it's incorrect to say that someone graduated college.

Example: Duffy graduated from Harvard.

Grateful/
Gratified

Grateful means "thankful." *Gratified* means "pleased."

Example: I'm grateful for the company's willingness to experiment with my idea.

Example: I was gratified by your speedy response to my request.

Had/Had of   *Had of* is wrong. Always.

Example: If I had read the memo, I wouldn't have been surprised by Nanette's resignation.

Half/Half of   Use *half* by itself when modifying a noun. Use *half of* to modify a pronoun.

Example: Half the people [n] at the convention skipped the keynote presentation.

Example: Only half of those [pron] who attended liked the speaker.

Hanged/Hung   *Hang* is the present tense and refers to all instances of hanging—pictures, laundry, or people. In the past tense, *hanged* is used to refer to people and *hung* to everything else.

Example: In the Old West, criminals were hanged.

Example: The painters hung the pictures after they finished their work in Lisa's office.

Home/Hone   *Home* means "move toward a target." *Hone* means "sharpen or whet." There is no instance in which the phrase *honed in* is correct, no matter how many times we see it in the newspaper or hear it on television. Think of a homing pigeon circling; it is *homing in* on its destination. It's not sharpening anything.

Example: The boss really homed in on marketing's responsibility for the project's failure.

Example: Jack honed his sense of humor at his colleagues' expense.

Imply/Infer   The speaker *implies*. The hearer *infers*.

Example: Richard implied that John stole the exams.

Example: From what Richard said, I inferred John was guilty.

Incredible/
Incredulous   *Incredible* means "astonishing or unbelievable." *Incredulous* means "skeptical or disbelieving."

Example: The sale Kim made was incredible. We were all incredulous when she told us how much money she'd made for the company.

Infinite/
Infinitesimal   *Infinite* means "without limit." *Infinitesimal* means "tiny." It is not the superlative form of infinite.

Example: The computer spit out an almost infinite set of data permutations.

Example: After studying the permutations, we realized that only an infinitesimal number of them were germane to our project.

Ingenious/
Ingenuous
Ingenious means "clever or resourceful." *Ingenuous* means "unsophisticated or guileless." *Disingenuous* means just the opposite: "insincere or crafty."

Example: Cameron thought up an ingenious method for sharing the data quickly.

Example: Sherri is so ingenuous people sometimes underrate her abilities.

Example: Fred's apology to Ivan was disingenuous, and everyone knew it.

In lieu of/
In light of
In lieu of means "in the place of." *In light of* means "because of."

Example: We'll agree to a barter arrangement in lieu of cash payment.

Example: In light of the new information, we've changed our projections.

Inter-/Intra-
Inter- means "between two or more entities." *Intra-* means "within one entity."

Example: XYZ Corporation is an interstate company that does business in New England.

Example: XYZ Corporation is an intrastate company that does all its business in Minnesota.

Irregardless/
Regardless
Regardless means "without regard," and *irregardless* would thus mean "without

without regard," which obviously makes no sense. Erase *irregardless* from your brain and your vocabulary. Most people who use *irregardless* probably are confusing it with *irrespective*, which has its own set of confusions.

Irrespective/ Respective	*Irrespective* means "not taking into account." *Respective* means "belonging to each individually."

Example: The boss announced that bonuses would be awarded irrespective of salary grade.

Example: Please go to your respective offices. We'll deliver the bonuses to you there.

Jail/Prison	*Jail* is a place of incarceration for those awaiting trial or not yet convicted of a crime. *Prison* is a place of incarceration for those who have pleaded guilty or been convicted.

Example: Phil spent the night in jail before his arraignment.

Example: He was later convicted of fraud and sentenced to three years in prison.

Jibe/Jive	*Jibe* means "agree." *Jive* either is a kind of music or means "kid" (v).

Example: His story didn't jibe with the facts.

Example: Jared is the town's expert on jive.

Example: Don't jive me, man. Did we really get the gig?

Justifiably/   *Justifiably* means "able to be justified."
Justly   *Justly* means "deserved or appropriate."

Example: Willie was justifiably annoyed that no one in the carpool ever offered to pay for gas.

Example: Was the embezzler justly punished when he received only ten months in prison?

Killed/Kilt   *Killed* is the past tense of *kill*. A *kilt* is a pleated skirt of tartan wool. Davy Crockett "kilt him a bar," but he's the exception.

Example: Until she learned about proper watering, Eve killed every houseplant she put on her desk.

Example: David looks imposing in a kilt.

Kudos   *Kudos* is a singular noun that means "praise for something one has accomplished." Because of the *s* on the end, the word appears to be plural, with the singular being *kudo*. However, there is no such word as *kudo*.

Example: Kudos to Jack for his incredible work on the fund-raising drive.

Last/Latter   *Last* means "coming after all others in a group of three or more." *Latter* means "second of two."

Example: Operations was the last department to turn in the figures that Hilary requested.

Example: Floyd and Lloyd were both considered for the promotion, but the latter received the nod.

Lay/Lie

There is more confusion over *lay* and *lie* than almost any other word pair in English. People are so confused it's now not uncommon to hear, "I lied down for an hour." Some folks think that people lie and things lay. That's an interesting memory device, but it's wrong. Things lie all the time, for example, *the calculator was lying on the desk*.

Let's take it one step at a time.

Lay means "to put or place" and always takes an object. *Lie* means "to recline" and never takes an object.

Example: I had to lay my book [object] aside when the doorbell rang.

Example: I was getting ready to lie down when the doorbell rang.

The past tense of *lay* is *laid*. The past tense of *lie* is *lay*.

Example: I laid the papers [object] in the chair, but now I can't find them.

Example: I was so tired I just lay around the house all day.

The participial form of *lay* is *laid*. The participial form of *lie* is *lain*.

Example: I had just laid my watch [object] on the bureau when I heard the noise.

Example: I'd lain down only a few minutes when I heard the noise.

The key to the *lay/lie* issue is whether there's a direct or indirect object involved in the sentence. If something—or even someone—is being put or placed, use *lay*, *laid*, *laid*. If a person or thing is simply hanging around in a recumbent position, use *lie*, *lay*, *lain*.

Of course, *lie* can also mean telling an untruth. In that case, the forms are *lie*, *lied*, *lied*. And *lay* can be used as a noun having to do with sexual contact, as in, "She's a great lay," but I don't recommend this usage around the office.

Example: I cannot tell a lie.

Example: I lied then, but I'm telling the truth now.

Example: I've lied to you again and again.

Lectern/
Podium

Lectern means "stand that holds a speaker's notes." *Podium* means "pedestal or platform." A speaker stands *behind* a lectern and/or *on* a podium.

Example: The keynoter laid her notes on the lectern, which was on a raised podium in the center of the room.

Lend/Loan

Lend (past tense *lent*, with participle *has lent*), which is a verb, means "give something to someone else temporarily." *Loan*, which is often used as a verb but is more properly a noun, is the thing that has been given temporarily. Got it? Many people say, "Will you loan me . . . ?" and the gods of usage don't frown, but "Will you lend me . . . ?" is correct, and the *lend/loan* distinction is one some people like to preserve. There's nothing wrong with being right.

Example: I'll be glad to lend you my scanner.

Example: I lent the scanner to Wynne.

Example: The loan of the scanner saved Wynne hours of research time.

Liable/Libel/ Slander

Liable means "held legally responsible for." It can also mean "likely." *Libel* means "publish false statements that damage someone's reputation." They are pronounced differently, *liable* having three syllables and *libel* only two. *Slander* means "utter a false statement with intent to damage another's reputation."

Example: The newspaper was held liable for the libel it printed about the mayoral candidate.

Example: The candidate is liable to sue the paper.

Example: The tabloids feel free to libel famous people.

Example: I heard all of Jerry's slander about Beverly, but I didn't believe any of it.

Like/Say

Please, if you are over the age of sixteen, do not use the word *like* to mean *said* and do not use it as a modifier if you don't need a modifier. "And then I'm like furious and he's like upset so I'm like ready to forgive him and she's like, 'Are you crazy?' and he's like, 'Are you going to listen to her?' and then we were all like totally bummed," is abysmal, and you sound as if (not *like*) you have a case of arrested development.

Luxuriant/
Luxurious

Luxuriant means "characterized by profuse growth." *Luxurious* means "very comfortable or extravagant."

Example: The CEO's view of the luxuriant gardens was the best thing about her office.

Example: This is the most luxurious yacht I've ever seen.

Memento/
Momento

In English, there is no such word as *momento*. Remember that a *mem*ento brings *mem*ories to mind, and you'll never mispronounce it.

Militate/
Mitigate

Militate means "have influence." *Mitigate* means "soften."

Example: Her terrible grammar militated against her being chosen for the job.

Example: Sue's rejection of the idea was mitigated by the tactful way she turned it down.

Moot/Mute

Moot (pronounced the way it looks) once meant open to debate or undecided. A more modern meaning also has arisen: no longer worth debating or talking about. *Mute* (pronounced *myoot*) means silent or not producing speech.

Example: Whether Ray had entered into a valid contract was a moot point.

Example: Whether the bill is accurate is moot; the customer has already paid it.

Example: Ray stood mute when his boss questioned him about the contract.

More than/
Over

More than refers to number; *over*, to spatial relationships. Although this distinction is giving ground and probably will disappear soon, it's a nice one and makes your speech a little sharper.

Example: There were more than four thousand employees at the recognition event.

Example: The event producer arranged for a hot air balloon to fly the Employee of the Year over the party.

Nauseated/
Nauseating/
Nauseous

Nauseated means "feeling ill"; *nauseous* means "causing nausea." Although they are often used interchangeably, there is a significant shade of difference between them. In fact, if you're *nauseous*, you're not sick yourself—you're making other people sick.

Example: I was so nauseated I had to cancel my meeting.

Example: The meat was nauseous [or, more commonly, nauseating]; I took one bite and sent it back to the kitchen.

Off/Off of

Don't use *off of*; *off* is sufficient.

Example: Please take the file folders off the credenza.

On behalf/
In behalf/ — *On behalf* means "taking the place or standing in for another." *In behalf* means "in the interest of another."

Example: She received the award for her volunteer work in behalf of the homeless.

Example: I'm here on behalf of my business partner.

Operated/
Operated on — "Denise was operated Monday morning," sounds as if the surgeon pulled Amy's strings to make her move. The correct usage is *operated on*.

Example: What time will the surgeon operate on Denise?

Oral/Verbal — *Oral* means "having to do with the mouth" or "spoken." *Verbal* means "related to written or spoken words."

Example: We had only an oral contract.

Example: The verbal portion of the contest required entrants to write an essay and give a speech.

Ordinance/
Ordnance — *Ordinance* means "rule or decree." *Ordnance* means "military weapons."

Example: The city council passed an ordinance about what ordnance could be stored at the old armory.

Orient/
Orientate — *Orient* means "locate in space" or "acquaint with a new environment." Although this process is called *orientation*, there is no

need to add another syllable to the word *orient*. It doesn't make you sound any more impressive. Although the British commonly use the word *orientate*, American usage prefers *orient*.

Example: We'll orient six new board members during the next week.

Noisome/Noisy   *Noisome* means "foul or objectionable." *Noisy* means "loud."

Example: What is that noisome stench?

Example: When all the printers are running at once, it's too noisy to think.

Notate/Note   We *note* or *take notes* or *make notations*, but careful speakers don't *notate*. Like *orientate*, *commentate*, and *administrate*, *notate* may sound more important, but nothing is gained by adding an extra syllable, and you run the risk of being considered stuffy as well as wrong.

Example: Please note the attendance at this meeting; I expected the entire staff to show up.

Example: Esmé took careful notes at the seminar.

Example: Her paper was full of mathematical notations no one could decipher.

Pacific/Specific   *Pacific* means "peaceful," and it's the name of a large ocean. *Specific* means "distinguished from others."

Example: The meadow evoked a pacific feeling.

Example: Sara found the specific paragraph she needed for the brochure.

Penultimate/   *Penultimate* means "next to last." *Ultimate*
Ultimate   means "last or final." *Penultimate* does *not* mean something more than the ultimate, because there *is* nothing more than the ultimate.

Example: After two hours of nonstop pontificating, the speaker finally reached his penultimate point; then we had to listen for another half hour before he reached his conclusion.

Example: After hours of work, we arrived at the ultimate solution.

Percent/   *Percent* requires a number; *percentage*
Percentage   follows an adjective.

Example: Ten percent of the people who voted mismarked their ballots.

Example: An overwhelming [adj] percentage of the shareholders were women.

Peremptory/   *Peremptory* means "not allowing disagreement or refusal." *Preempt* means "to appropriate or displace."
Preempt

Example: The boss does nothing but issue peremptory commands.

Example: The president's visit preempted the usual staff meeting.

| Perquisite/ Prerequisite | *Perquisite* means "payment in excess or instead of salary," such as a bonus, a tip, or an extra week's vacation. It's sometimes referred to as a *perk*. *Prerequisite* means "something required as a condition of something else." |

Example: Franklin thought the perquisites of the job were more important than the salary.

Example: Having an MBA is a prerequisite for being considered for this position.

| Phenomena/ Phenomenon | *Phenomena* is the plural of *phenomenon*. It is not correct to say, "This phenomena . . ." |

Example: The hurricane was a terrifying phenomenon.

Example: Some phenomena that occur in nature cannot be recreated in the laboratory.

| Picture/ Pitcher | *Picture* means "graphic representation of people or things." A *pitcher* is a lipped container that holds liquids or the baseball player who throws the ball to the batter. |

Example: The staff photographer took a picture of Juliet holding one of the pitchers we manufacture.

| Poisonous/ Venomous | *Poisonous* means "containing or having the effect of poison." *Venomous* means "capable of injecting venom." |

Example: The company was sued for inadvertently selling some poisonous mushrooms.

Example: We work with venomous snakes to develop some of our pharmaceuticals.

Practicable/ Practical	*Practicable* means "able to be accomplished." *Practical* means "useful or suitable."

Example: Emma's solution was the most practicable because it required no additional resources.

Example: Emmett's sales ideas are always practical because he spent so many years in the field offices and knows what the sales staff needs.

Precede/ Proceed	*Precede* means "place before in time, space, or rank." *Proceed* means "begin or continue an action."

Example: Professor Jones preceded Professor Smith in the graduation processional.

Example: Even though Professors Jones and Smith are still at the graduation, let's proceed with the faculty meeting.

Prescribe/ Proscribe	*Prescribe* means "advise the use of a medicine" or "lay out a course of action." *Proscribe* means "forbid."

Example: The doctor prescribed an antibiotic for Sue's pneumonia and proscribed any activity for three days.

Preventative/ Preventive	*Preventive* and *preventative*, both adjectives, mean "concerned with preventing." Although *preventative* appears in some dictionaries, *preventive* is greatly preferred.

Example: The soldiers had a series of inoculations as a preventive measure.

Prone/
Supine

Prone means "lying face down." *Supine* means "lying face up."

Example: The victim lay prone in the hallway.

Example: We placed the patient in a supine position.

Prostate/
Prostrate

The *prostate* is a gland found at the base of the urethra in male mammals. *Prostrate* means "lying face down or overcome with exhaustion."

Example: Ralph was almost prostrate after the all-night meeting.

Example: The doctor examined Ralph's prostate.

Raise/Rise

Raise means "make higher." *Rise* means "become upright or erect." These words follow the same rules as *lay* and *lie*. *Raise* always has an object; that is, something must be raised. *Rise* never takes an object; something rises.

Example: Raise your hand [object] if you're taking the field trip.

Example: Please rise for a moment of silence.

Rational/
Rationale

Rational (pronounced *RASH-o-nal*) means "reasonable or sane." *Rationale* (pronounced *rash-o-NAL*) means "basis for a course of action."

Example: Terence gave the most rational explanation for management's new directives.

Example: He fully understood management's rationale for making the changes.

Real/Really   *Real* is an adjective and means "existing in fact" or "genuine." *Really* is an adverb and means "in truth" or "positively." Therefore, *it was a real nice party* may be acceptable in informal speech, but it's incorrect in formal usage. *Nice* is an adjective, and adjectives are modified by adverbs. *It was a really nice party* is correct.

Example: Is this a real diamond?

Example: Lorelei is really interested in becoming a gemologist.

Rebut/Refute   *Rebut* means "argue against." *Refute* means "prove a statement or opinion is wrong." You can rebut someone all day without ever refuting his point of view.

Example: Logan rebutted every suggestion about relocating the offices.

Example: The attorney was able to refute Lorna's recitation of the facts.

Receipt/Recipe   *Receipt* means "written acknowledgment of payment." *Recipe* means "directions for preparing a dish." As an example of the changeable nature of English, *receipt* also used to mean *recipe*, but that meaning has fallen out of favor.

Example: Did you get a receipt for the computer repairs?

Example: Helen always omitted one ingredient when she shared a recipe.

Recoup/
Recuperate

Recoup means "recover what one has lost or its equivalent." *Recuperate* means "recover from illness."

Example: Jim was able to recoup his losses in the stock market with real estate investments.

Example: It will take Jim six weeks to recuperate from his knee surgery.

Recur/Reoccur

Recur means "happen again." There's no need to lengthen it to *reoccur*.

Example: Eugenie's proofreading mistake recurred in every draft of the report.

Regime/
Regimen/
Regiment

Regime means "the government in power." *Regimen* means "specially prescribed course," often related to diet and exercise. *Regiment* means "military unit with two or more battalions." Although these three words come one after the other in the dictionary, they are miles apart in meaning. Use them carefully.

Example: The Watergate scandal occurred during the Nixon regime.

Example: My doctor placed me on a strict regimen of calorie counting.

Example: Will more than one regiment be sent into battle?

Regrettable/
Regretful

Regrettable means "something to be regretted." *Regretful* means "having feelings of regret or being sorry." They are closely related, but have quite different shades of meaning.

Example: Ian's drinking too much at the company picnic was a regrettable lapse in judgment.

Example: Ian was regretful about his behavior—and hung over, too.

Reluctant/
Reticent

Reluctant means "unwilling." *Reticent* means "discreet or inclined to shield one's thoughts or feelings."

Example: We were reluctant to leave for the seminar without Jean.

Example: Dale is reticent about discussing her relationship with Roy.

Restaurateur/
Restauranteur

Restaurateur means "proprietor of a restaurant." Even though the second spelling, which includes the word *restaurant*, seems logical, most dictionaries and word usage mavens call it a variant or an error. Some online dictionaries with aural pronunciation guides list *restauranteur*, but then pronounce it without the *n*. You should, too.

Revert/
Revert back

Revert means "go back to an old habit or condition." The prefix *re-* means "back" or "again," so *revert back* is redundant. The same goes for *return back*, *refer back*, and many other words with the *re-* prefix.

Example: When she was under stress, Julia reverted to smoking.

Example: Edward returned home when the meeting was over.

Example: Wendy referred to Peter's earlier sales presentation to prove her point.

Rightfully/ Rightly
Rightfully means "owned or held by a just claim." *Rightly* means "correctly."

Example: The business was rightfully hers by the terms of her father's will.

Example: She rightly believed she'd been cheated when the court awarded the business to her husband.

Scare/Scarify
Scare means "frighten." *Scarify* means "mark the skin," often resulting in a scar.

Example: We were scared of the boss's reaction when we discovered we'd gone over budget.

Example: Primitive tribes sometimes scarify themselves during puberty rites.

Sensual/ Sensuous
Both of these words mean "related to the senses," but *sensual* refers more often to bodily sensations, particularly those related to sex, whereas *sensuous* usually refers to aesthetics.

Example: We're publishing a very graphic adult book on sensuality.

Example: We're publishing a beautiful coffee-table book on the sensuous pleasures of fine dining.

Serve/Service   *Serve* means "work for," "provide goods or services to customers," or "meet the needs of another." As a verb, *service* means "maintain." It also has a meaning in animal management, which is to bring the stud to the female. Perhaps to sound more self-important, many businesses have dropped *serve* in favor of *service*, for example, *we service our customers one at a time*. This usage conjures up interesting mental images, some of them obscene. When you're talking about people, use *serve*.

Example: We're proud of the way we serve the public.

Example: We're proud of the way we service your car.

Example: The farmer was proud of the way his bull serviced Bossy.

Set/Sit   *Set* means "put or place." *Sit* means "place one's body in an upright position"; for people, that means resting on one's buttocks. Like *lay* and *raise*, *set* requires an object. Something must be set. Like *lie* and *rise*, *sit* never takes an object. Things sit.

Example: Please set the computer on the desk in the other office.

Example: Come sit by me. We have so such to talk about.

Should have/ Should of	The phrase *should of* has no meaning and is never correct. It arises because the contraction *should've* (which stands for *should have*) sounds very much like *should of*. The same confusion arises with *could have* and *would have*. When you pronounce *have* clearly, the listener has no doubt that you know what you're saying.

Example: Elmer should have avoided the intraoffice squabble.

Shrink/ Shrank/ Shrunk	The present tense is *shrink*. The past tense is *shrank*. The past participle is *shrunk*. Follow the same format for *drink, drank, drunk* and *sink, sank, sunk*.

Example: Did Pat's vast ego shrink when the boss yelled at him in the meeting?

Example: Honey, I shrank the kids [no matter what the film is called].

Example: Our revenues have shrunk over the past two years.

Example: Can I get you something to drink?

Example: He drank a whole bottle of water in less than fifteen seconds.

Example: Give me the keys. I can't let you drive when you've drunk so much.

Example: Did the enemy forces sink the submarine?

Example: The safe containing the bonds sank into the river.

Example: The ship had sunk after being torpedoed.

Silicon/
Silicone

Silicon is a nonmetallic element widely found in the earth. *Silicone* means "any organic silicon compound." Be careful not to refer to the *Silicone Valley* unless you mean surgically enhanced cleavage.

Example: The device used a silicon chip.

Example: Is silicone safe for use in the body?

Sneaked/
Snuck

Sneaked is still preferred. Although you'll find *snuck* in some dictionaries as an informal or colloquial expression, those same dictionaries continue to list *sneaked* as the past tense of *sneak*.

Spade/Spay

A *spade* is an implement for digging in the earth. *Spay* means "neuter a female cat or dog." The past tense of *spay* is *spayed*, not *spaded*.

Example: I spaded the garden for several hours.

Example: Last week we had our puppy spayed.

Suit/Suite

Suit (pronounced *soote*) means a matched set of clothing. A *suite* (pronounced *sweet*) is a set of rooms or furniture. Don't interchange these words and talk about living-room suits, unless you mean a set of clothes you wear only in the living room.

Example: Paul bought a new wool suit.

Example: Paulette bought furniture for her new office suite.

Tack/Tact

Tack means "course of action or direction." *Tact* means "a keen sense of what to do or say in order to avoid giving offense."

Example: Jack said the team needed to take a different tack to solve the sales problem.

Example: Harry was famous for his tact and courtesy.

Taunt/Taut

Taunt means "provoke or jeer at." *Taut* means "pulled tightly."

Example: Holly taunted Merry for the misspelled headline in the advertisement.

Example: We pulled the table drape taut before we set out the brochures.

Tax refund/
Tax return

A *tax refund* is what you receive when you've overpaid the government. A *tax return* is what you file with the government. You spend your refund, not your return.

Example: I'm going to use my tax refund for a new desk chair.

Example: Did you file your tax return on time?

Than/Then

Than is used in comparisons. *Then* refers to time or order.

Example: I'd rather be safe than sorry.

Example: We'll go to the bank and then to the airport.

There are/
There's

There's an unfortunate tendency for advertisers—and many others—to use *there's* followed by a plural, for example, *there's hundreds of reasons to shop here*. That's an incorrect usage. *There's* means *there is* and it requires a singular.

Example: There's not one flaw in this prototype.

Example: There were hundreds of bugs in the earlier model.

Tortuous/
Torturous

Tortuous means winding or twisting. *Torturous* means agonizing.

Example: His reasoning was tortuous.

Example: Her migraine was torturous.

Toward/
Towards

They're both right, although you'll more likely hear *toward* in the United States and *towards* in Great Britain.

Try and/Try to

If you're attempting to accomplish something, say *try to*.

Example: Bill will try to finish the analysis by this afternoon.

Venal/Venial

Venal means "able to be corrupted." *Venial* describes a sin that's not so serious as to endanger one's soul.

Example: Greg is the most venal politician in the state, but views his corrupt practices as only venial transgressions.

Wet/Whet   *Wet* means "soaked with liquid." *Whet* means "sharpen." Be aware that something does not *wet* your appetite. Your mouth may be watering, but *whet* is the word you're after. Sound the *h* to differentiate the two.

Example: Competition whets Hayley's creativity.

Example: When the dock sank, we all got wet.

AND SINGLES, TOO

At   *At* is a lovely preposition, but don't put it at the end of a sentence. I know everybody did it in the sixties, but it was wrong then and it's wrong now. *Where's it at?* is still considered substandard English. *Where is it?* serves the purpose adequately.

Au jus   *Au jus* means "with [*au*, pronounced *oh*] its natural juices [*jus*, pronounced *zhoos* or *zhoo*, but not *juice*]." *Au jus* is not a thing; it's a description. *With au jus* means "with with juice." That's redundant—and repetitive, too. And incorrect.

Example: Let's have the lamb *au jus*. I've heard it's delicious here.

Lifeflighted   There is no other instance in which the word *flighted* would be correct, and it's wrong here, too. People are transported to the hospital by helicopter or airlifted.

Nother   *Nother* is not a word. Don't say "a whole nother thing." Use *other* instead.

Only

Only can be a tricky word. Place it as close as possible to the word or words you want to highlight.

Example: *Only* Paul did the illustrations. [Paul worked alone. There were no other illustrators.]

Example: Paul did *only* the illustrations. [Although Paul provided the artwork, he didn't do any of the writing.]

Perfect

Perfect, like *pregnant*, *dead*, or *unique*, has no comparative or superlative. Something cannot be *more perfect* than something else, nor can it be the *most perfect*. Just *perfect*.

Save off

This phrase is a favorite of advertisers, but it's redundant and can be confusing. You either *take 20 percent off* the price or *save 20 percent*, but you don't *save 20 percent off*.

Thusly

This word is unnecessary. *Thus* works just fine.

To be

To be is an important infinitive. Imagine if Shakespeare had removed *to be* from Hamlet's famous soliloquy. The first line would read simply, "Or not?" Eliminate from your speech all such sentences as *this work needs done*, *these supplies need ordered*, or *this desk needs fixed*. They make no sense. Proper usage dictates *this work needs to be done*, *these supplies need to be ordered*, or *this desk needs to be fixed*. If you want to avoid confusion, just say, "I'm going to do the work," "Please order the supplies," or "Ask maintenance to fix the desk."

If you don't want to use the infinitive, recast the sentence altogether.

To coin a phrase

To coin a phrase means "to invent a word or phrase." Do not use this expression if you really mean you're about to spout a cliché. For example, saying *to coin a phrase, we need to get our ducks in a row* is incorrect because there's nothing new in the coined phrase. Unless you actually invent a new phrase, there are very few instances in which *to coin a phrase* is apt.

Turned up missing

Something either turns up or it's missing. You can't have it both ways (see also *went missing*).

Unique

Never say something is *more unique, most unique,* or *very unique.* It's either unique or it isn't. Period.

Ways

Ways is a fine word if you're using it to mean *methods* or *means.* However, tacking the *-s* on as a suffix in words such as *anyways* is wrong. The word is *anyway.*

Went missing

Television reporters like this phrase, so you'll often hear that a person *went missing* a few days ago, presumably as a result of foul play. This usage is nonsensical; the appropriate substitute is *disappeared* or even *vanished.*

Where

Where, of course, refers to a point, place, or position. *Wheres* is not a word, nor is it a suffix, so eliminate *anywheres, nowheres,* and *somewheres* from your speech. *Anywhere, nowhere,* and *somewhere* work just fine.

3

DE-MANGLING COMMON EXPRESSIONS AND DE-DANGLING MODIFIERS

Misusing a well-known expression won't get you fired, but it might get you laughed at and ridiculed. If it's a one-time error, join in the laughter, but be sure to fix the problem the next time you utter the phrase. However, if people snicker whenever you open your mouth, it's best to review your use of idioms. Being the office joke will not propel you to the top of the pyramid. Here are some often-jumbled phrases:

YOU SAID *WHAT?*

Another thing coming	The correct expression is *another **think** coming*.

> **Example:** If Rae thinks she's going to take credit for my work, she has another think coming.

A pit in my stomach	The correct expression is ***in the** pit of my stomach*.

Saying that something gives you a pit in your stomach makes it sound as if you've swallowed a peach. The pit of the stomach is below the breastbone in the area of the solar plexus. If someone hits you there, it takes your breath away. And that's often the way you feel when something affects this region of the body.

Example: When I realized the report contained outright lies, I had an uneasy feeling in the pit of my stomach.

Could care less   The correct expression is **couldn't care less**. If you *could* care less about something, it means you still care. If you *couldn't* care less, then you really don't care at all.

Example: Do you want to eat first or finish the report now? I couldn't care less.

Doggy-dog   The correct expression is *dog-**eat**-dog*. It means "very competitive."

Example: In our department, it's a dog-eat-dog world, and it's no fun.

To (or for) all intensive purposes   The correct expression is *to (or for) **all intents and** purposes*. It's a redundant phrase, but if you're going to use it, be sure to do so correctly. It means "in every important way."

Example: To all intents and purposes, this prospectus is finished.

In like Flint   The correct expression is *in like **Flynn**. There are various explanations for the meaning of this phrase, which means that one has a privileged position. Some people think it has to do with the late Errol Flynn's prowess in bedding women. Others theorize that it derives from Boss Flynn, a New York Democratic Party leader during Franklin Roosevelt's presidency, who was so powerful that any candidate he backed automatically won. The confusion probably arises from a comedy called *In Like Flint*, in which James Coburn played a James Bond–like agent.

Example: After dinner with the boss, Gary was in like Flynn.

Road to hoe   The correct expression is *row to hoe*. This expression comes from farming. We hoe rows of crops, not asphalt.

Example: Once Sam left the department, Joanne had a tough row to hoe.

The proof is in the pudding   The correct expression is *the proof of the pudding is in the eating*. It's somewhat related to *you can't judge a book by its cover* and means that appearances may be deceiving. You don't know if the pudding's any good until you eat it. This is an old expression, possibly dating back to the twelfth century. It took twentieth-century speakers to render it useless.

Example: Dale looks like an honest businessman, but the proof of the pudding is in the eating. We'll watch to see if he handles the next deal ethically.

Tongue and cheek   The correct expression is *tongue in cheek*, which means *facetious* or *in jest*. If people want to indicate they're kidding, they may place their tongues against the inside of their cheeks. Tongue-in-cheek statements are meant to be humorous and are often sarcastic.

> **Example:** You shouldn't have believed me; I was speaking tongue in cheek.

POSITIONING WORDS FOR SUCCESS

Modifiers are words or groups of words that limit or describe other words. Two bad things can happen to modifiers: they can be misplaced or they can dangle. A misplaced modifier modifies the wrong word or phrase. A dangling modifier seems to modify nothing at all—it's just out there, looking for something to do.

Modifiers that don't work can be funny. Almost every grammar text includes a few giggle-producing examples. If you're not going for laughs, however, misplaced or dangling modifiers can make you sound as if you didn't think things through. Here are some prime examples—enjoy!

If you take advantage of our special offer, you can have our unique eye surgery for eighteen months at zero interest. I don't know about you, but I don't think I'd survive surgery that lasted for eighteen months, and if I were the client I wouldn't have paid for this ad. How about this instead? *If you take advantage of our special offer, you can have your surgery now and pay no interest for eighteen months.*

Under fire for statements she made to the press, Henry Horner terminated his secretary. Henry appears to be gender confused, but his secretary is definitely out of a job. Or possibly sleeping with the fishes. Clean it up this way: *Henry Horner fired his secretary for statements she made to the press.*

Why did Jack interview in a brown tweed suit with a bad haircut? Oh, lighten up. Even the best suit can have a bad hair day. But the sentence would be improved by revamping it: *Why didn't Jack get a decent haircut and wear a different suit to the interview?*

The dog's coat was the color of tea with a tail that wagged incessantly. It's so hard to get that wagging tail into the cup! Make the sentence more understandable this way: *The dog, whose tail wagged incessantly, had a coat the color of tea.*

At the last committee meeting, we discussed resurfacing the access roads with the township trustees. Wow! Those trustees are tough. Most municipalities resurface with asphalt. The sentence works better like this: *At a joint meeting with the township trustees, the committee discussed resurfacing the access roads.*

Our product kills most of the germs that cause illness in as little as fifteen seconds. Those germs work fast, don't they? Here's the cleaned-up version: *In as little as fifteen seconds, our product kills most of the germs that can cause illness.*

Why pay a florist hundreds of dollars only to have them wilt in less than a day? The florist will certainly be angry when those dollars start to droop. Let's put some flowers into this sentence and look at the result: *Why pay a florist hundreds of dollars for flowers that will wilt in less than a day?*

The victim was found in the car with a bullet hole in the chest. Were the medics able to stop the flow of transmission fluid? *Found in his car, the victim had a bullet hole in his chest* would be a little less confusing.

The businessman was accused of punching a coworker in the 1700 block of Main Street. Better than punching him in the eye, I guess.

Using the latest high-tech tools, the solution was discovered. This sentence says that the solution used the high-tech tools, but in fact, someone else did. So this example might be restated: *Using the latest high-tech tools, our scientists discovered the solution.*

Finishing the article, the subject was still confusing. Once again, the modifier is modifying the wrong word. It appears that the subject finished the article; since that's impossible, we must find out who the reader is and put him into the sentence, like this: *After finishing the article, Jeremy still found the subject confusing.*

Finding his photo, there was no reason to look further. In this instance, the phrase *finding his photo* needs to modify a noun or pronoun that indicates who's acting: *Once we found his photo, we didn't need to look any further,* or *Having found the photo, we stopped looking.* In both cases, putting a subject pronoun—*we*—into the sentence makes things much clearer.

In casual speech, the placement of modifiers is usually not as precise as it is in formal conversation, so it's not something to fret over in social situations. If you're preparing a speech or presentation, however, you need to pay attention to modifiers so your audience won't groan.

Not every goofy turn of phrase involves a dangling or misplaced modifier. Some confusion may result because the speaker inserted an unnecessary, inappropriate, or incorrect word. Here are some examples ripped from the airwaves, presentations, and conversations.

The president unleashed a negative attack. We'd all agree that positive attacks are more pleasant, but they'd lose a little pizzazz, wouldn't they?

The CEO of our company was originally born in St. Louis. He was later born again in Prague, Yellow Knife, San Francisco, and Moline. *He was born in St. Louis* is sufficient.

The artist was interred for six years in a Siberian work camp. But they couldn't bury his spirit. The word the speaker should have used was *interned*.

A member of the Beatification Committee will present the award to the president of the Garden Clubs, whose members planted more than two thousand bulbs at the city gate. Clearly, they were saints for planting all those flowers, but I think the speaker meant *Beautification Committee.*

The group held its semiannual Valentine's Day fund-raiser. We all love love, but Valentine's Day comes only once a year.

The singer spent her entire adolescence literally in a fish-bowl. That must be where she developed her amazing breath control. *Figuratively* is the right word.

Keep modifiers as close as possible to the words they modify and check the meaning and placement of every word.

AND JUST ONE MORE THING: THE MIXED METAPHOR

A metaphor is a figure of speech in which one image is substituted for another: *an acre of ignorance, a mountain of misery, an explosion of invective.* Metaphors can be powerful if they are consistent: *He swam in an ocean of money, but drowned in the undertow of debt* presents two water images that work well together.

However, mixed metaphors offer multiple images that fight one another. The result is a confusing mass of words that don't say much. Here are some examples:

Mixed metaphor: John was bogged down in a storm of controversy.

Better metaphor: John was buffeted by the storm of controversy.

Mixed metaphor: Caught in a web of lies, the boss called the bet.

Better metaphor:	Caught in a web of lies, the boss struggled to free herself from disgrace.
Mixed metaphor:	Let's give the idea a test run before we jump into the pool.
Better metaphor:	Let's give the idea a test run before we put it on the fast track.
Mixed metaphor:	He was always running upstream against the crowd.
Better metaphor:	He was always swimming against the current of public opinion.
Mixed metaphor:	Stunned by the barrage of criticism, Roderick pulled in his horns.
Better metaphor:	Stung by the fusillade of criticism, Roderick withdrew to nurse his wounds.

Many "mixed metaphors" aren't really metaphors at all, but common expressions that have been combined in ways that often are laughable. Here are a few:

- He speaks with a fork in both sides of his mouth
- She's not the brightest bulb in the pencil box
- Jack was up a tree without a paddle
- She's colder than ice on a witch
- They've got the monkeys over a barrel

When making a comparison, make sure the things you're comparing work well together. Precision pays if you want to sound smart.

PRONOUNS, MOOD SWINGS, AND FINDING YOUR VOICE

PRONOUNS

Self-quiz: Please circle the number of any sentence that is incorrect.

1. Everyone should bring their assessment forms.
2. Can you meet with John and I on Tuesday?
3. Listen to Gary and myself on the podcast.
4. Her and Harrison are in charge of the entire project.
5. Somebody left their cell phone in the conference room.
6. Dad and him founded the company.
7. Just between you and I, the manager is an idiot.
8. Give the report to both she and her supervisor.
9. Jenny herself approved the final report.
10. If you have questions, just call Jill or I.

Only Number 9 is correct, so if every other answer isn't circled, you need a brush-up on how to use pronouns properly. Unfortunately, to understand why we make mistakes with pronoun usage, we are forced to revisit (gasp!) some rules of grammar.

Defining Our Terms

A pronoun is a word that substitutes for a noun. Personal pronouns refer to specific persons, places, or things, and they come in three forms, or cases: the nominative (or subjective) case, the objective case, and the possessive case (see table 1).

Table 1. Personal pronouns

	Case		
	Nominative, or subjective	Objective	Possessive
Function	serves as subject of sentences	serves as direct object, indirect object, or objects of prepositions	indicates ownership
Examples	*I, you, he, she, it, we, you, they*	*me, you, him, her, it, us, you, them*	*my/mine, your/yours, his, her/hers, its, our/ours, your/yours, their/theirs*

In written English, possessive pronouns can create a lot of havoc because of ghastly misspellings such as *their's* or *its'*. In speech, however, these types of errors don't create a problem. They can be seen but not heard. The big issue in spoken English is misuse of the other two forms.

Subjective Opinions and Object Lessons

Most people use subjective and objective case pronouns correctly if there's only one subject or object. Take a look at these examples:

- *I* will pick up Rita at the airport.
- *They* are going to work together on the product launch.
- *We* salespeople need to present a united front.
- Please let *me* know when you're going to the airport.
- We will work with *them* on the product launch.
- They treated *us* salespeople shamefully.

So far, so good. Once we get beyond one subject or one object, however, logic seems to fly out the window. Subjective and objective pronouns get churned up together in a sort of linguistic stew that not only sounds awful, but also makes no sense. Here are some stunningly bad examples of subjects and objects gone wrong.

- **Him and Fred *have become good friends.*** Because it's an objective pronoun, *him* cannot be used as the subject of a sentence; the correct choice is *He and Fred*.
- *If you need directions, e-mail **Milly or I**. I* is a subjective pronoun; it can't be used as a direct object; the correct choice is *Milly or me*. Some people believe that using *I* in this context elevates their speech. In fact, the reverse is true.

Prepositions, which are a big cause of pronoun mistakes, are words that show relationships in space, time, or position (see the "cheat sheet" on p. 100). Some of the most frequently used prepositions are *with, of, to,* and *for*. A prepositional phrase is a phrase that begins with a preposition, and the noun or pronoun that completes a prepositional phrase is called a prepositional object. If the prepositional object is a pronoun, it must be in the objective case. Speakers who don't know this rule are likely to spout such unattractive and incorrect sentences as the following:

- *Is it possible **for you and I** to meet next week? For* requires an objective pronoun. *Is it possible for you and me to meet?* is correct.

- *The photographer took a picture **of he** and Julie for the company handbook.* Of must be followed by an objective pronoun, which in this instance is *him*. *The photographer took a picture of him and Julie* is correct.
- *The president's invitation came only **to Bill and she**. To* is the preposition; *her* is the correct prepositional object. *The president's invitation came only to Bill and her* is right.
- *We went to the employee recognition dinner **with they** and their friends.* The preposition *with* takes the objective case: *them*. *We went to the dinner with them and their friends* is the right way to say it.

A Cheat Sheet of Prepositions

Above	Beside(s)	Into	To
Across	Between	Like	Toward(s)
After	Beyond	Near	Under(neath)
Against	By	Of	Until
Among	During	On(to)	Up
Around	Except (for)	Out	Upon
Before	For	Over	With
Between	From	Since	Within
Below	In(to)	Through(out)	Without

If you have a question about which pronoun is correct in a sentence with more than one subject or object, here's a test. Take out the conjunctions *and* or *or* and every other subject or object until you're left with only the pronoun you want to test. Then read the sentence. You'll be able to tell immediately if your choice is right. If it's not, substitute the other case and try again.

Me and Bud will produce the event. Take out *and Bud*. Now the sentence says *Me will produce the event.* Not likely. So *Bud and I* is correct. (*I and Bud* is pompous. It's always polite to let the other person precede you in a sentence. Think of it as holding the door open and allowing someone else to go first.)

Give the event schedule to Jim or I. Test it by removing *Jim or* from the sentence. You're left with *Give the event schedule to I.* No. Give it to *Jim or me.*

Using two e-mail addresses makes it easier for Kylene and me to keep track of the project. To check this sentence, remove *Kylene and.* The sentence now reads *Using two e-mail addresses makes it easier for me to keep track of the project,* and that's the correct use of the pronoun.

Call she or Jack to make changes to the schedule. Remove *or Jack.* What's left is *Call she to make changes to the schedule.* You wouldn't say that, would you? *Call her or Jack* works.

We're going to the warehouse with he or Quintina and the supervisor. Take out *or Quintina and the supervisor.* The remainder of the sentence now reads *We're going to the warehouse with he,* and you know that's not right. *Him* is the correct choice.

He and his brother kept the company from going bankrupt. Remove *and his brother.* What remains is *He kept the company from going bankrupt.* That's right.

Interesting Case 1: Pronouns following Than

Pronouns that come after the word *than* can be a special problem. Sometimes subjective pronouns are called for; sometimes objective pronouns are necessary. It all depends on the speaker's meaning. For example, see the following sentences:

- *He cares more about making money than I.* This sentence means that he cares more about making money than I do.
- *He cares more about making money than me.* In this case, he cares more about making money than he does about me.

Most of the time, mistakes in pronouns following *than* involve using the objective when the subjective is what the sentence calls for. The incorrect sentences sound like this:

- He's been with the company longer than *me*.
- He makes a bigger salary than *her*.
- She's older than *him*.

If you have doubts about which pronoun to use, finish the sentence mentally, and your doubts will disappear for good.

- *He's been with the company longer than **me** (has).*
- *He's been with the company longer than **I** (have.)*
- *He makes a bigger salary than **her** (does).*
- *He makes a bigger salary than **she** (does).*
- *She's older than **him** (is).*
- *She's older than **he** (is).*

Interesting Case 2: Either *and* Neither

Since *either* and *neither* always involve two options, and some of the options may be plural as well, it makes sense to think they'd require a plural verb. The fact is that both of these words are singular, and they always take a singular verb.

- Neither of the speakers *was* very dynamic.
- Either of the vice presidents *is* eloquent when speaking to the media.

However, when *either* and *neither* are used as pairs, as in *either . . . or* and *neither . . . nor*, they are no longer pronouns but rather correlative conjunctions (that's a term you may forget if you wish), and they take a singular or plural verb based on the subject, usually a noun, closest to them, as in the following:

- Neither the president nor the board members *are* coming.
- Neither the board members nor the president *is* coming.

- Either the students or the instructor *is* confused.
- Either the instructor or the students *are* confused.

It can be hard to remember which pronouns to use when you're in the act of speaking, so spend some time studying the rules and practicing out loud. If you've been misusing particular pronouns for years, the correct forms can sound bizarre until you're used to them.

I once watched a reporter doing a live shot from a horrifying multicar accident; she compounded the disaster with her agonizing on-air mental search for the right pronoun. The expression on her face was painful to watch as she struggled to come up with the correct word—and then made the wrong choice. Practice takes away the sense of unfamiliarity and gives you greater assurance in speaking; it wires the new words into your synaptic network and helps avoid the frozen expression that comes over your face when you're on the spot and trying to decide which option to choose.

Myself, Me, *and* I

Pronouns ending with -*self* are either *reflexive* or *intensive* pronouns. That is, they refer to a previous subject and tell us that the same person or thing is being talked about. Intensive pronouns bring attention to a noun or pronoun that's already been used and usually follow the noun or pronoun immediately:

- I *myself* believe the sales figures are inflated.
- The CEO *himself* showed up at Harriette's retirement tea.

Reflexive pronouns refer to the subject of the sentence and also share in the action of the verb. They usually follow the verb.

- I hurt *myself* when I ran into the file cabinet.
- I'll go over to accounting *myself*.
- You should discuss this issue with marketing *yourself*.

Many people abuse the -*self* pronouns by using them where they are not necessary, and when these pronouns are misused, the result is abominable sentences like the following:

Be sure to distribute the data analysis to Elaine and **myself**. *Myself* is used incorrectly. For *myself* to work here, it would have to be preceded somewhere in the sentence by *I*—and there is no *I* to be found. Therefore, you should say "to Elaine and me."

Randy or **myself** *will take your reservations for the conference. Myself* is used incorrectly as a subjective pronoun. The correct pronoun is *I*.

Myself *and my family thank you for this great award.* This sentence is a mess all the way around. First, *myself* should not be used as the subject pronoun. The correct choice is *I*. The subjects are also inverted. Speakers should put themselves last in any list of other people they mention. This sentence should read *My family and I thank you.*

Speakers may resort to the -*self* pronouns because they are unsure about whether to use a subjective or objective pronoun, and choosing a third option relieves them of having to make the decision. You can almost hear their thought process: "Hmmmm. Do I say, 'Order your office supplies through Eve and *I* 'or 'Eve and *me*'? Neither one sounds right. I'll just say *myself*."

Some experts believe that people avoid the pronouns *I* and *me* because they think *myself* sounds somehow more weighty, elevated, and important, or alternatively, that saying *I* or *me* is rude and boastful. That's just silly. No one listening to the proper use of first-person pronouns would believe the speaker to be either too timid or too grandiose. However, those whose ears are assaulted by an incorrectly used *myself* may believe the speaker to be uninformed or ignorant.

Definitely Indefinite

Most personal pronouns are straightforward: *I*, *you*, *he*, *she*, *him*, *her*, *we*, *us*, *they*, *them*. However, a few of them, called the indefinite pronouns, don't refer to a specific person. They can cause bewilderment because some are singular, some are plural, some are switch-hitters, and it may be hard to remember which is which (see table 2).

Table 2. Indefinite pronouns

Always singular	Always plural	Context-dependent
anyone, anybody, anything, each, either, everybody, everyone, everything, neither, no one, nobody, nothing, somebody, something, someone	both, few, many, other, several	all, any, most, some, none

Indefinite pronouns can bollix up something called antecedent-pronoun agreement. Before you start searching for your eighth-grade grammar text, here's a quick review. An antecedent is a word or group of words to which the pronoun refers. When the antecedent is also a pronoun, the two pronouns must both be singular or both be plural:

- *He* put *his* watch on the lectern.
- *She* finished *her* work early and went home.
- *They* should have abandoned *their* project weeks ago.
- *We* should send *our* suggestions to the CMO herself.

The same rule applies if the antecedent is indefinite. When the rule is disregarded, interesting sentences result. Here are some typical examples:

- *Everybody* should bring *their* company rosters.
- *Anybody* has a right to *their* own opinion.

- *Someone* who wants to advance should keep *their* wits about them.

Strictly speaking, these sentences are wrong. All of them have singular antecedents and plural pronouns. In the olden days, there was no question about how to fix a sentence like this. A singular antecedent was followed by *his* (*Everyone should bring his calendar*), which obviously is singular, but also clearly male.

With the coming of the women's movement, however, considerable protest arose about excluding more than half the population from the world of pronouns. Some language mavens concocted inventive and often dreadful solutions to the problem—*s/he* and *s/him* leap to mind. Writers often solved the problem by alternating *he* and *she*, *his* and *hers*, and *him* and *her* in their prose, but that option didn't work well in spoken English.

Most people finally agreed that *he or she* and *his or her* was the easiest way around the issue (*Everyone should bring his or her calendar and roster*). That works fine for uncomplicated sentences, but it gets Byzantine if the sentence is more complex. *Everyone should bring his or her roster if he or she needs to check his or her personal directory against the master list* is enough to tie anyone's tongue in a knot, and it sounds inane.

In response to this tortuous way of expressing themselves, speakers began to substitute *their* even if the antecedent pronoun was singular. Strict grammarians flinched; the more liberal wing of the group was quicker to accept the change. The fight rages on, with those on both sides beaning each other with stylebooks, but this is a case in which usage eventually will win out over the rules of grammar. It won't happen overnight, but it will happen. *Their* is gender-neutral, and its use has precedent even in the writings of Shakespeare.

Today, however, there are still folks around who know the old rules, and in the business setting it's best to err on the side of caution and use the pronouns properly. If a sentence will become too cluttered by doing so, you can dispense with the problem by making everything plural, unless the group is exclusively one sex (*Those who are going should bring **their** PDAs*; ***Each** woman has a right to **her** own opinion*; ***Every** **guy** who's coming to the retirement bash for old Joe should bring **his** own beverage*).

You can also substitute the second person *you* for other pronouns. *If you're coming to the meeting, bring your PDA.* All these constructions work very well and are acceptable to both women and grammarians. The he/she debate highlights the flexibility of English, and the next issue demonstrates how confusing that flexibility can be.

Pick a Number

The verb in a sentence must agree with its subject in number—singular or plural. Therefore, when a singular indefinite pronoun, such as *anyone*, is the subject, the verb must also be singular. A plural indefinite pronoun such as *several* must be accompanied by a plural verb. That's relatively easy to figure out, but the pronouns that are context-dependent are another story.

The context-dependent pronouns are singular in some cases and plural in others. If you are talking about something that can be counted (computers, coffee mugs), use the plural:

- *All* the file folders *are* color-coded.
- *Some* of the investment-grade coins *were* missing.
- *Are* there *any* doughnuts left?

However, if what you're discussing cannot be counted or divided (water, cement), use a singular verb:

- *All* the freight *was* delivered to the wrong warehouse.
- *Some* of the meeting *will be* devoted to financial issues.
- *Is* there *any* coffee left?

None is a bit trickier than some of the other indefinite pronouns. If you mean *not one single thing or person*, it's singular. It's also singular if the noun that follows it is singular. If the noun that follows is plural, then *none* takes a plural verb.

- As a protest, *none* of the vice presidents [not one of them!] *is* going to the staff meeting.
- *None* of the food at this conference *is* fit for human consumption.
- *None* of the donation *was given* to the charity.
- *None* of the speeches *were* very inspiring.
- *None* of the coins *were* rare.

THE MOOD SWING

There's something in English called the subjunctive mood, and it determines which form of the verb *to be* we choose: *was* or *were*. A sentence in the subjunctive mood frequently starts with the word *if*, which makes the sentence a conditional statement. If the conditional statement is contrary to known fact, use the subjunctive *were*; if the statement is true, use the indicative *was*. In addition, if the sentence expresses a hope or wish that hasn't come true, use *were*:

- If I *were* more senior in the company [which I'm not], I would be in line for the promotion.
- If I *were* guilty of fraud [which I'm not], I'd take my punishment.
- If she *was* speaking at the seminar [and she was], her session was over before I arrived.
- If the program *was* good [and it was], the food was even better.
- I wish I *were* taller. I can't see the speaker very well.

Most people don't know what the subjunctive mood is, let alone how to use it. But now you do, which puts you, if not in a class by yourself, at least in one with very few members.

HEARING VOICES

What's the difference between these two sentences?

> The CFO's administrative assistant embezzled $25,000 from the firm.
>
> A $25,000 embezzlement by the CFO's administrative assistant has been discovered.

The first is in the active voice. The subject of the sentence—*the administrative assistant*—has performed an action. The second is in the passive voice. The subject—*a $25,000 embezzlement*—is acted upon. Notice the words *by the*; that usage is almost always a tip-off that the sentence is in the passive voice.

Business relies far too much on the passive voice, and a couple of reasons explain its popularity. Using the passive helps Nervous Nellies and Nelsons avoid accountability for their actions; passive voice subtly shades the truth, giving cover to those who choose to avoid scrutiny. The need for this behavior can be traced to a business climate that demands instant results and flawless performance. Since neither is possible, the passive provides a place for the actor to hide, double shuffle, and pass the buck to unnamed others.

The passive voice is useful if you really don't know who carried out a particular action, for example, *In the morning, the safe was found to be open.* Some usage specialists also believe the passive is appropriate if the action is more important than the person who carries it out, for example, *The candidate's résumé is being scrutinized carefully.* However, I believe this justification for the passive can be problematic. Who decides whether the actor should be hidden from view? In the example above, who's scrutinizing the résumé, the hiring committee or a counterterrorism task force? The vagueness of the passive makes it ideal for evading or obscuring facts. On a few occasions, that sort of avoidance may be necessary, but in most cases it isn't.

The passive can be especially detrimental in customer service operations. How would you like to hear these messages on your voice mail?

- "Your complaint was reviewed by our service desk and found to be without foundation."

- "It has been discovered that your account is in arrears."
- "Your order has been lost."

No one appears to be responsible for any of these untoward events, and the customer is frustrated because she has little, if any, recourse. There's no one to talk to about what to do next. The actors are faceless and unavailable. In the first example, the actor isn't even human. An unknown but apparently very intelligent desk has made a customer service decision. It would be much better for client relationships if someone were to step out from behind the rocks, take the blame, and get on with solving the customer's problem:

- "Ms. Adams of our customer service department has reviewed your complaint. Since it's been more than ninety days since your purchase, we're unable to refund your money without the receipt. However, we'll be happy to issue a store credit."
- "Your account is overdrawn. Please make an immediate deposit to cover the overdraft and fees. If you'd like to consider adding overdraft protection to this account, Mr. Cohen will be happy to help you. Please call him at (614) 555-5555."
- "A member of our staff misplaced your order. We apologize for the inconvenience and are sending the merchandise by express mail at no cost to you."

These active voice messages deliver the same bad news as those in the passive. The customer is not getting his money back, the bank account is still overdrawn, and the merchandise will be late. However, forthright messages like these may save the relationship because the customer is not left to twist in the wind. Think about that when you're tempted to weasel out with the passive.

PART TWO

SOUNDING SMART AT WORK

5

SAY WHAT YOU MEAN

Nearly everyone agrees that business English is in a state of disrepair. Companies are hiring consultants to teach employees how to write simple declarative sentences and paragraphs that make sense. Jargon-filled columns litter the Web, and novelty companies sell T-shirts and mugs that skewer impenetrable office communication. Buzzword Bingo and Dilbert help employees blow off a little steam as they deal with the frustration of trying to get things done in an atmosphere in which no one knows what anyone else is saying. It's funny—but then again, it isn't.

Corporate English used to be a little stuffy, but at least it was understandable. Two major factors have conspired to change that situation: a need for speed, coupled with a desire to avoid accountability.

With a few exceptions, today's business climate does not tolerate a strategic, long-term view. What matters is next quarter's profits. Investors buy in, expect immediate results, and jump out quickly if they aren't satisfied. They have scant patience with earnings numbers that don't outpace Wall Street's expectations every single quarter. A miss of only two to three cents may result in an exodus of disgruntled investors. Rather than viewing an occasional less-than-stellar quarter as a normal part of the business cycle, they pick up their marbles and go home, often doing a great deal of damage to the companies they abandon.

Xerox president and CEO Ann Mulcahy says that the emphasis on short-term performance is "dysfunctional" and that many CEOs would like to say, "'I don't care and I'm just focused on the long term, but the pressure is extraordinary.' If I could take Xerox private, I'd do it yesterday."[1]

It's no big surprise, then, that the communications coming from corporate America are clouded in business-speak and riddled with static. To keep investors from stampeding, business spokespeople must present as rosy a picture as possible, even if the situation is dire.

As he stands in front of his shareholders, the CEO doesn't say the company is going under for the third time; it is simply "seeking the protection of Chapter 11 of the bankruptcy code." Caught by a television crew, the CFO does not mention fraud; she speaks only of a few "bookkeeping irregularities," for which the offenders have not been fired. Rather, these former officials have left, apparently voluntarily, to "seek other opportunities." All too often lately, the new opportunities have included the chance to don those fetching orange jumpsuits. Shading the truth may help people keep their jobs, but in the long term, refusing to use plain English to report bald facts causes more harm than good. Obscuring reality has cost business the public's respect. Equally important, corporate America is losing the regard of its employees. In a 2005 survey, only 40 percent of American workers said that they trusted top management always to communicate honestly, and only 38 percent said management did a good job of explaining important decisions.[2]

This lack of trust leads to less employee *engagement*, which happens to be a hot new buzzword. Lack of engagement means that fewer employees are willing to shoulder duties not explicitly spelled out in their job descriptions, or, as buzzmeisters like to say, they don't exert any "discretionary effort." Why would they, if they don't trust management? Part of the reason for this distrust can be laid at the feet of managers who speak only corporate lingo, which often consists of arcane, incomprehensible jargon.

Jargon has a useful place in business. For those in the same profession, technical jargon makes conversation quick and efficient. But the jargon that now dominates so much of general business communication has the opposite effect, isolating those who speak from those who hear and insulating the speaker from ever being held accountable for what he has said. After all, if one has never stated an intelligible opinion, one is never answerable for it.

Businesspeople also are afraid to speak clearly for fear of litigation. Trailblazing lawsuits have been instrumental in helping to eliminate sexist jokes, racist language, and other inappropriate forms of workplace communication, but their success has also emboldened some employees to spend more time filing grievances than working. The threat of having to deal with specious suits for imagined slights can divert company officials from the important tasks of running the business; the timidity engendered by fear of litigation has, in many cases, dampened purposeful discourse and led many businesses to adopt vapid, vacuous language that has nothing going for it except that it's innocuous. And in a time when anything can be litigated, using a lot of words to say nothing may save money. However, the cumulative effect is ultimately damaging. As we tamp down our language to avoid responsibility and keep things placid, we communicate less well, and as our communication falters, American business becomes less able to compete. We waste time because we don't understand one another, and we waste money because miscommunication results in false starts that must be corrected. Design failures, reorganization snafus, product recalls, and many other untoward consequences can be the result of poor communication, especially spoken exchanges.

Spoken English carries a burden that written English doesn't. Without a text to refer to, listeners are likely to misunderstand what they hear. Therefore, what we say must be clear and unambiguous. That doesn't mean every word has to be baby-simple and devoid of the curlicues and grace notes that make English such an interesting language, but it does mean that our choice of words should be carefully considered. We must make it as easy as possible for our listeners to understand and remember what we say.

Unfortunately, however, instead of concentrating on clarity, we have created a language rife with pretentious phrases that obfuscate rather than simplify. Such choices are intended to telegraph the superiority of those who use them. But creating an in-group necessarily creates an out-group as well, and communication between the two can falter as resentment builds.

Many of today's business buzzwords—*scalability*, *stickiness*, and *bandwidth*, to name a few—are part of the jargon of the computer industry, where they have actual meaning. However, most of what we hear today, whether borrowed from the computer industry or any other, is devoid of sense or intelligence. Here's a recent example from a sales executive for a manufacturing company:

> We're proud to announce that we've entered into a strategic alliance with Consolidated Ball Bearing and Screen Door, Incorporated. We're in agreeance that this new synergistic enterprise will allow us to deliver best-in-class services, value-added solutions, and optimal go-forward plans that will drive results to the bottom line.

Huh? No one within the sound of the speaker's voice had the foggiest notion what she said. The statement is fuzzy, boring, and virtually incomprehensible. Words have been spoken, but nothing has been communicated. How about this instead:

*Name of the company changed to protect the speaker's reputation.

> We're proud to announce a new partnership with Con-
> solidated Ball Bearing and Screen Door, Incorporated.
> Together we'll be able to provide better service than
> ever before. We'll be adding three new product lines,
> and sales of those products will increase our net
> profits approximately 35 percent.

It's crisp, clean, and buzzword-free, and the speaker has stated
the company's expectations with precision.

To avoid descent into a hell of gobbledygook, it would be
wise to expunge trendy, inflated expressions from your vocabulary. All the examples in table 3 were taken from real sources
—from print pieces to audio presentations to television interviews to the World Wide Web—which means they are widely
used. When you have to think about substitutions, it may surprise you to learn how much you lean on the latest buzzwords—and how that makes you sound.

Table 3. Bad busswords and better replacements

Awful business buzzword	Example	What it means	How to replace it
Accountability	"The job accountabilities are spelled out in detail in the manual."	Responsibility	"The manual outlines your responsibilities."
Actionable	"All of these steps are reasonable and actionable at this point in time."	Take action, make progress, work on. (The real meaning of the word *actionable* is "giving a cause for legal action." If that's what you mean, go ahead and use it. Otherwise, choose something else.)	"We can make quick progress on every one of these steps."
Action items	"There are seventeen action items on the agenda."	Things to do, things requiring action, or things to act on	"The agenda lists seventeen items we need to act on today."

Agreeance	"Do you think we can finally get to agreeance today?"	Agreement (Why did someone think that coining the word *agreeance* served any purpose, and why did anyone else adopt it?)	"Will the committee agree on a course of action?"
Ahead of/behind the curve	"Are we behind the curve vis-à-vis others in our competitive space?"	Leading/Lagging	"Are we behind our competition in getting to the market?"
At the end of the day	"At the end of the day, the lawyers couldn't get the job done."	Finally, ultimately	"Ultimately, the legal team failed to prove the case."
Back in the day	"Back in the day, we took our customers' complaints seriously."	Before, formerly	"We used to take customer complaints more seriously, and I think we should give greater attention to them today."

Awful business buzzword	Example	What it means	How to replace it
Backsource, homesource	"We outsourced our IT functionalities, but found we were losing control and wasting money, so we backsourced."	Bring a job back in house	"It was cheaper to hire foreign workers to handle our customer service, but we got so many complaints we reopened the customer service operations in this country."
Ballpark	"Can you give me a ballpark estimate?"	Approximate	"What's the approximate cost?"
Bandwith	"We don't have the bandwidth to handle a project of this magnitude."	Ability, capability	"This project is beyond our capabilities."
Best-in-class/ best-of-breed	"We generate and implement best-in-class financial solutions."	Best, superior	We provide superior investment services for every client."
Best practices	"We have studied best practices in seminar design and have embedded them in all our courses."	Most effective methods	"We have developed the most effective seminars you'll find anywhere at any price."

Term			
Bleeding-edge	"This program is so bleeding-edge we don't know if all the bugs are worked out, but we're going to ship it anyway, along with a list of known defects and possible workarounds."	Products that are so new they aren't perfected yet	"We're pretty sure this program doesn't work as well as it could, but customers want it anyway. We'll sell it now and provide upgrades later."
Blocking and tackling	"We have to focus on blocking and tackling before we can make big plays in advertising."	Basic functions	"We have to make sure we've ironed out our customer service problems before we invest in a big advertising campaign."
Blue-sky thinking	"Let's use this time to do some blue-sky thinking about recapturing our clients' mindshare."	Imagination, creativity	"We need to be more creative than we've ever been to take back the number one position in our market."
Circle back	"We'll circle back to this subject at the end of the meeting and loop everyone in."	Discuss again	"Let's return to this topic at the end of the meeting to make sure everyone understands what the plans are."

Awful business buzzword	Example	What it means	How to replace it
Competitive set	"How are we positioned against the competitive set?"	Competitors, competition	"Is the competition beating us again?"
Connect the dots	"Can we connect the dots and arrive at a universally agreed-upon solution?"	Figure something out	"Have we figured out how to get everyone to agree?"
Content provider	"Let's talk to our content providers to make our communications more competitive."	Writer, director, graphic designer	"Please call a meeting with the writer and graphic designer. Our competitors' ads look much better than ours, and they seem to be more effective, too."
Core competency	"Our core competency is designing innovative solutions for high-net-worth clients who want to create trusts."	Specialty, what we do best	"Our specialty is creating innovative trusts for wealthy clients."
Critical path	"We can't have any deviation from critical-path functions."	Appropriate steps, systematic approach	"We must execute every step of the plan flawlessly to make our deadline."

Term	Example	Plain meaning	Example
Customer-centric	"We pride ourselves on customer-centric service."	Focus on the customer	"Our focus is always on what's best for the customer."
Deep dive	"Our deep-dive research told us to drop our lowest-cost product."	To examine in depth, to conduct research	"Our extensive customer surveys proved that our lowest-cost product was a loser."
Deliver	"We deliver customized solutions for every client."	Offer, provide	"We provide services geared to every client's unique needs."
Deliverable	"Our deliverable for the meeting is due by close of business today."	What we promised to do	"We promised every committee member a set of recommendations by next week."
Download	"I'll download everything about my position functionalities to you before I leave the company."	Give information	"I'll tell you everything you need to know about my job before I leave the company."
Drill down	"How far shall we drill down to reach the level of detail the project requires?"	Research, study in greater depth	"How much research do we need?"
Drive	"What factors will drive your decision-making process?"	Have an impact on, affect, cause	"What factors will influence you to choose our team?"

Awful business buzzword	Example	What it means	How to replace it
Driver	"Consumer behavior is the major driver of our research."	Impetus, cause, reason	"Consumer behavior is the reason for everything we do."
E-anything	"We have a new, integrated e-commerce solution."	Online, Web-based	"You can now buy directly from us online."
Empower	"We empower every employee to make decisions at the point of customer interface."	Give responsibility to, trust	"We trust all our employees to make on-the-spot decisions in favor of our customers."
End-to-end	"We'll provide an end-to-end solution."	From start to finish (*End-to-end* has some meanings specific to various computer protocols, but the phrase, like many others, has made it into mainstream business-speak and been watered down to mean nothing.)	"We'll handle the installation from beginning to end."

End users	"We design everything we do with the end user in mind."	Customers	"We keep customers' needs front and center in all our planning."
Enterprise	"All of our solutions are enterprise based and synergistic."	Company, corporation, business	"Let's think about what's best for the entire corporation, not just for individual divisions."
Escalate	"I'm going to escalate you to one of our customer service managers."	Take a problem to the next level of management	"I'm going to put one of our customer service managers on the phone with you."
Facilitate	"The handbook should facilitate your familiarity with our new structure."	Make it easier, help	"The handbook will make it easier for everyone to understand the new structure."
Functionality	"Does this program have chart-creation functionality?"	Ability, function	"Can I use this program to create charts?"
Gain traction	"This idea is never going to gain any traction."	Become accepted	"No one is ever going to accept this idea."

Awful business buzzword	Example	What it means	How to replace it
Get one's arms around	"I can't get my arms around the complaint resolution solution."	Understand	"I don't understand how we resolve customer complaints."
Go-forward basis	"We'll try the new methodology on a go-forward basis."	In the future, move ahead	"We'll try the new design for the next six months, and then we'll evaluate it."
Granularity	"In our research project, we drilled down to a very fine level of granularity."	Detail	"Our research was extremely detailed."
Grow down	"Finance will be looking at ways we can grow down our losses."	Lessen, decrease	"We have to figure out how to decrease our losses."
Headcount	"What's the headcount in this component of the enterprise?"	Number of people	"How many people work in this division of the company?"
Heavy lifting	"Jeannette isn't fond of heavy lifting."	Hard work	"Jeannette's lazy and never helps anyone else."

Herding cats	"Honestly, trying to keep this bunch in line is harder than herding cats."	Managing	"This is a difficult group to manage because there's a lot of interpersonal conflict among staff members."
Human capital	"We invest heavily in human capital because it's our most important resource."	People	"We seek out the best people and pay them well."
Incremental	"Changing our data-capture methodology resulted in an incremental increase in productivity."	A small increase	"The newer methods have helped us increase our productivity 2 percent."
Inplacement	"We inplaced Joan from executive support to project management."	A transfer within the company	"We transferred Joan from executive support to project management."
Joined-up thinking	"We're all in agreeance that joined-up thinking is the only way to increase our presence in the sales space."	Cooperating, discussing ideas	"We all have to cooperate in finding ways to outsell the competition."
Knowledge management	"We have to increase our bandwidth in knowledge management."	Sharing information	"We have to do a better job of getting information to the right people."

Awful business buzzword	Example	What it means	How to replace it
Knowledge transfer	"We all hoped the seminar would bring about a significant knowledge transfer, but the experience was less than optimal."	Teaching and learning	"Nobody learned anything at the seminar. The leader was unprepared and the material was outdated."
Learnings	"There are learnings to be gleaned when a project of this magnitude doesn't achieve its projected success."	Lessons	"The project's failure taught everyone a big lesson."
Level-setting	"Let's have a level-setting meeting before the go-forward plans are set in cement."	Making sure everyone understands	"Let's have a meeting to be sure everyone knows what our plans are."
Leverage	"We have to leverage our human capital and our cutting-edge solutions to realize incremental gains to our bottom line."	Use to our advantage	"We must use all our employees' talents to develop new profit-making products."
Living assets	"Our living assets were the drivers behind our 180-degree shift in management style."	Employees	"Our employees demanded better treatment from management."

Term			
Low-hanging fruit	"We think our competition's failings may make their best customer low-hanging fruit."	Easy opportunity	"Our competition messed up, and we think we can snatch their best customer from them."
Messaging	"We're looking to improve our messaging."	Messages, advertising, public relations, communication	"We need to make our communication more effective."
Methodology	"Our methodology involves being proactively anticipatory regarding our customers' needs."	A way of doing things	"We impress customers by tracking their usage patterns and anticipating their next order."
Metrics	"We're performing very well against our metrics related to customer care."	Standards, measures of performance	"Our research says we're doing a better job in resolving customer complaints."
Mission critical	"Every aspect of this project is mission critical."	Essential, fundamental	"There's no room for error in this project. Everything must be perfect."

Awful business buzzword	Example	What it means	How to replace it
Off-peopling	"Off-peopling will result in a workplace we can't imagine today."	Replacing people with automated systems, automation	"Ever-increasing automation will radically change the workplace and the workforce."
Off-shoring	"To realize bottom-line efficiencies, we off-shored all our manufacturing functionalities to China."	Moving various business processes to a place where labor is cheaper	"Our company has moved manufacturing to China."
On a (daily, weekly, monthly) basis	"You're accountable to ensure that this function is carried out on a daily basis."	Daily, weekly, monthly	"You have to complete this task every day."
On our radar screen	"The launch of the competition's new product is definitely on our radar screen."	We are aware	"We know when, where, and how the competition will be introducing their new product."
On the runway	"Rob's idea is on the runway, but I don't think it will gain enough traction with management."	In development	"Rob's developing his idea, but I don't think management will accept it."

Open the kimono	"Do you think we can trust our potential partners enough to open the kimono now?"	Share critical information	"We have to share some confidential data if we want the partnership to work."
Outcome-based	"Our outcome-based approach means we concentrate on quantifiable, measurable parameters in developing our contracts."	Measurable	"When we write a contract, we include measurable objectives that our clients can use to check our progress."
Out of pocket	"I'll be out of pocket for a week."	Not able to be reached, away from the office (*Out of pocket* has a real business usage. It means expenses employees pay for themselves; e.g., "The meals were an out-of-pocket expense, but I'll be reimbursed for them next month." The phrase has expanded in recent years, and the explanations for why that's happened are not particularly sensible.)	"I'm on vacation next week, and I'm not taking my cell phone or my computer. You can't reach me. Don't try."

Awful business buzzword	Example	What it means	How to replace it
Out of runway	"The brochure project is out of runway."	Missing the deadline	"The brochure won't be printed on time, and that means it will be useless."
Out of the box	"To develop innovative products requires everyone to utilize out-of-the-box thinking."	Original, creative	"We need your most original and creative ideas to create new and desirable products."
Out of the loop	"Jack is always out of the loop, and it's holding him back."	Uninformed	"Jack never knows what's going on in the company, and it's holding him back."
Ownership	"We expect our employees to take ownership of decisions made in their departments."	Responsibility	"Employees in every department are responsible for their own customer service decisions."
Paradigm shift	"Voting out the entire board of directors represented a paradigm shift on the part of formerly acquiescent shareholders."	Big change	"The shareholders woke up, decided the company needed to go in a new direction, and voted out the CEO and the board of directors."

Parameter	"What are the parameters of the project we should consider before we begin?"	Aspect, quality, property (In fact, *parameter* does not mean any of these things, nor does it mean "boundary." That's a *perimeter*. A *parameter* is a constant in an equation, but it has become acceptable in informal speech to use *parameter* to mean a limiting factor. It might be wise to choose another word in formal speech.)	"What are the most important aspects of this project?"
Ping	"I'll ping you about the meeting tomorrow."	Get in touch with, call, e-mail	"I'll call you in the morning."
Planful	"We are planful in our approach to innovation."	Careful in planning	"Every innovation is carefully planned."

Awful business buzzword	Example	What it means	How to replace it
Platform	"Our platform includes state-of-the-art technology combined with customer-centric service."	Belief, standards	"We demand that our staff maintain the highest standards of customer service."
Point in time	"At this point in time, we have no idea how the pension fund was depleted."	Now, then, in the future, currently	"Right now, we don't know who drained the pension fund, but we're beginning an investigation."
Populate (an idea)	"We're populating this idea through focus groups."	Try an idea out on different people or groups	"We're testing the idea with focus groups."
Portal	"Our Web site serves as the portal to our array of product offerings."	Entry point	"Just enter our Web site to view all of our products."
Presenteeism	"Presenteeism is resulting in more employees getting sick."	Showing up for work when you're ill	"If you have the flu, please stay home so you don't make others sick."

Pushback	"You can anticipate some pushback from employees on the new sick-time policy."	Resistance, questioning	"Employees will dislike the new sick-time policy."
Push the envelope	"Let's push the envelope in developing our new tires."	Innovate, experiment	"Let's experiment with several new ideas before we decide on which tire we'll manufacture."
Ramp up	"We'll ramp up for production for the next fiscal year." "We'll ramp up our output of automotive product this year."	Prepare or increase	"We'll be ready to introduce the new tires within eighteen months." "We'll manufacture four hundred more luxury cars and five thousand more sedans this year."
Repurpose	"We repurposed the former cafeteria space as a creative-thinking facility."	Use in a new way, remodel	"We're remodeling the old cafeteria into a quiet place employees can use for creative thinking."

Awful business buzzword	Example	What it means	How to replace it
Reskill	"We have to reskill all the employees we deselected."	Retrain	"We should retrain the employees we were going to fire."
Results-oriented	"Our results-oriented approach is highly proactive."	Concerned with results	"We've found that concentrating on results is highly effective."
Rightsource	"The decision on rightsourcing several accountabilities will be made within the month; we will seek the correct balance between insourcing, outsourcing, and selective sourcing."	Decide whether employees or external vendors should handle specific functions such as information technology, printing, or human resources	"We've decided that it makes good sense to have our printing done outside the company."
Robust	"Our new software is more robust than ever."	Workable, loaded with features	"Our new software has more features than even we thought possible."

Term		Meaning	Example
Scalable	"The program is infinitely scalable."	Expandable, flexible	"The program is so flexible that it can be used in everything from a home office to an international network."
Seamless	"We have seamlessly integrated marketing communications and finance functions."	Smooth, easy	"The combined Marketing and Finance Department is working very smoothly."
Silo	"The operations silo is less productive than we anticipated."	Function, activity, department, division	"The Operations Division isn't functioning effectively."
Skill set	"Her skill set is more comprehensive than his."	Skills, abilities	"She has stronger skills than he does."
Sniff test	"This new retirement formula doesn't pass the sniff test."	Assessment, evaluation	"I've evaluated the retirement policy and found it favors management rather than long-time employees."

Awful business buzzword	Example	What it means	How to replace it
Solution	"Take a look at all our world-class (marketing/software/sales/PR/any other thing you can think of) solutions."	Ideas (*Solution* is a fine word, but if a problem is not stated, *solution* becomes a meaningless term. *Solution* is probably the most overworked word in the busines lexicon.)	"Let's give our customers some new ways to solve their problems."
Space	"We'll solution this issue in the sales space."	Arena, market	"We'll test this product in supermarkets and pharmacies."
State-of-the-art	"All of our products are state-of-the-art."	Newest, unparalleled, unequaled	"We bring you only the newest, most advanced products."
Suite	"We provide a full suite of financial services."	Group, range	"We offer a wide range of coordinated financial services."

Term			
Synergistic	"The new strategic partnership with our previous competitor is synergistic."	Mutually beneficial	"The new partnership with our previous competitor benefits both companies and all the shareholders."
Take offline	"Let's take the personnel issues offline."	Discuss outside this meeting or away from others.	"Let's meet privately about the personnel problems."
Tee up	"Shall we tee up the meeting?"	Begin	"Let's begin."
That said	"That said, he's a fine manager."	But, however	"He has some rough edges, but he's a fine manager."
Thirty thousand feet	"We should examine this idea from thirty thousand feet."	Bird's-eye view	"Let's examine all the possible ramifications of this decision."
360-degree	"Let's take a 360-degree look at this opportunity."	Comprehensive, wide-ranging, from every direction	"We need to look at this opportunity from every possible perspective."
24/7/365	"Our service staff is available 24/7/365."	Instantly available, anytime	"Call us anytime, day or night."

Awful business buzzword	Example	What it means	How to replace it
Upskill	"Wolfgang needs to upskill in the desktop design space."	To become more competent in a particular skill or group of skills	"Wolfgang needs to take some courses in desktop design if he expects to advance in this department."
Value add	"Our experience is a value add."	Something extra (This term means absolutely nothing unless you can pinpoint what the extra something is—and most people can't.)	"Our experience is a plus."
Value proposition	"Our specific value proposition is that we have more customers in your industry than anyone else."	What sets a business apart	"What makes us special is our vast experience in your industry."
Values-based	"Our values-based approach means you can trust us not to authorize changes you have not approved."	Ethical	"Our insistence on ethical practices means we won't authorize changes you haven't approved."

Viral marketing	"The new campaign has a strong viral-marketing component that should optimize its reach and effectiveness."	Marketing strategy that involves passing a message from person to person, usually by e-mail	"We hope the advertising message is strong enough that each reader will pass it on to every other person in her address book."
White paper	"We're issuing a white paper on the school-to-work initiative."	Report	"Our report will explain the school-to-work program in detail."
World-class	"We're a world-class company."	Exceptional, superb	"We're an exceptional company, and I'd stack us up against anyone else in the industry, here or abroad."
Worst-case scenario	"The worst-case scenario involves losing the bid."	Worst case	"In the worst case, we'd lose the bid."
Zero tolerance	"We have zero tolerance for weapons in the workplace."	Forbidden, unacceptable	"Don't even think about bringing a weapon into this office."

6

ELIMINATING FLABSPEAK

Buzzwords, although grating, are not the only disagreeable features of corporate speech. I've lumped the others under the heading of "flabspeak" because these habits of speech turn language flaccid, robbing it of its strength and power to communicate.

Flabspeak tends to be self-conscious, exclusionary, and devoid of meaning. Excessive use of it brands the speaker as an ill-spoken, unoriginal thinker who goes along with whatever linguistic fad is in fashion. However, the trouble with fads is that by definition they are self-limited. The words that are in today can be out tomorrow, and if you're still using phraseology that's passé, you run the risk of sounding not only insipid, but also out of touch. It's better not to lean on such weak, unstable crutches. Plain English works in any situation and serves both speaker and listener much better.

LET NOUNS BE NOUNS

Nouns are sturdy words that let listeners know what person, place, or thing is being discussed. Verbs are flexible and subtle, with various gradations of meaning. In English, many words serve as both nouns and verbs: *a shower* and *to shower*, *a mop* and *to mop*, a *shoulder* and *to shoulder*, and hundreds, perhaps thousands, more.

Sometimes nouns and verbs are differentiated only by an accent: *PERmit* and *perMIT*, *CONflict* and *conFLICT*, *UPset* and *upSET*, *FInance* and *fiNANCE*, *PROtest* and *proTEST*, *OBject* and *obJECT*. The noun forms are usually accented on the first syllable, and verb forms on the second.

Nouns often become verb forms over a period of time, and in today's world, many words related to technology seem to be moving that way. For example, *access* was once exclusively a noun. Today, the verb form, *to access*, is common, but many believe it should be restricted to technological use. That is, *we accessed the information online* would be acceptable, but *I accessed all my friends* would get a thumbs down.

In general, however, most of the nouns that have become business verbs today are hideous and serve no purpose. They are often confusing and do nothing to make language more effective or forceful.

Table 4 lists some verb forms to avoid and some substitutions that are more generally understood.

Table 4. Wretched verbs and how to avoid them

Wretched verb	Example	What it means	How to avoid it
To architect	"Rod will architect the new department."	To design a plan or specifications	"Rod will do the planning for the reorganization."
To circle-slash	"We've circle-slashed smoking in our buildings."	To forbid or outlaw	"We don't allow smoking in our headquarters."
To committee	"We'll committee your idea next week."	To discuss in committee	"The committee will talk about your idea next week."
To effort	"We're going to effort a sales blitz this weekend."	To try, attempt	"We're going to try to move the end-of-season merchandise with a big sale this weekend."
To flowchart	"Shall we flowchart the span of the departmental changeover?"	To draw a flowchart	"Let's make a flowchart to see how long the departmental change will take."
To helm	"Sara will helm the project."	To lead	"Sara will lead the project team."

Wretched verb	Example	What it means	How to avoid it
To hindsight	"Manuel will hindsight the results."	To review when a project is completed; to analyze	"Manuel will review whether we stayed on time and within budget."
To impact*	"How will the change impact the staff?"	To affect or have an impact on	"What impact will the change have on the staff?"
To interface	"Let's interface about this Monday."	To meet or call	"I'll call you Monday."
To language	"The most able leaders language themselves effectively."	To write or to say, to express oneself	"Great leaders speak and write well."
To maintenance	"We're going to maintenance these items for our affiliate."	To maintain or to store	"We're going to store these items for our partners because we have better security."
To matrix	"We'll matrix the new data."	To create or modify a matrix	"We'll put the new data into our matrix to see if they have an impact on our planning."

*This verb form is increasingly used, but there are some people who loathe it and will react negatively to those who use it incorrectly. And while we're at it, let's avoid the word *impactful*; although it loosely means that an action "has a significant effect," it's an ugly word that should be abandoned.

To office	"Ted is officed in Building Two."	To assign office space, to be located in an office	"Ted's office is in Building Two."
To podium	"We'll podium Sarah at the far end of the banquet hall." "With that time, Jake is sure to podium."	To stand or place on a podium; in Olympic years, to win a medal.	"We'll put Sarah's podium at the end of the banquet hall." "With that time, Jake's going to be on the winner's podium for sure."
To resource	"Can you resource this for us?"	To secure resources; to do research	"Please find out if we can hire more people or increase the budget for this project." "Could you research whether our engineers have applied for a patent on the new process?"
To solution	"We'll solution this in the afternoon meeting."	To find an answer or solution to a problem	"We'll look for answers this afternoon."
To source	"Let's source some consultants."	To find or look for	"Let's start a search for some good consultants."
To surface	"We should surface these concerns quickly."	To raise or discuss	"We should raise these issues right away."

Wretched verb	Example	What it means	How to avoid it
To task	"She will be tasking Matilda with the newsletter."	To assign	"She'll be assigning the newsletter to Matilda during the term of the project."
To topline	"Please topline me on your findings."	To share pertinent data	"Please give me the most salient data in your report."
To transition	"Rolf transitioned to the new department."	To make a transition	"Rolf made an easy transition to his new duties."
To trend	"We'll trend these figures."	To look for a trend	"We'll examine the figures to see if they indicate a trend."
To vision (or, God help us, visioneer)	"We'll vision the parameters of the solution at the next session."	To envision, visualize, find	"Let's see if we can find some way out of our financial problems."
To whiteboard	"I'll whiteboard your thoughts."	To write, summarize, gather, synthesize	"I'll summarize everyone's ideas on the whiteboard."

Beyond creating execrable nouns from lovely verbs is the reverse practice of turning a verb into a noun. It's not quite as prevalent, but it's just as unattractive. The most prominent of these transformed verbs today is *a disconnect*. This word is properly a verb meaning "to break a connection," usually electrical or telephonic. *We disconnected the computers during the electrical storm* is correct. *There's a disconnect between marketing and sales* isn't. Substitutions could include *a misunderstanding*, *a disagreement*, or *a difference of opinion*.

Another transmogrified verb, usually related to advertising, is a *spend*, which means how much is spent. *Budget* is a pleasant replacement.

Made famous by the Janet Jackson breast-baring incident at the Super Bowl a few years ago is the concept of *a reveal*. This word has been enthusiastically embraced by the makeover television shows as well. "After these words, stay tuned for the big reveal!" Couldn't we just say that Janet revealed too much? Or that we're going to reveal the results of our makeover? What's the point of creating a noun that's not necessary?

A common verb consistently misused in business is *grow*. *Grow*, except in the case of agriculture, is an intransitive verb, which means it has no object. In other words, we don't grow things; things grow. *We grow carrots, onions, and tomatoes at our farm* is acceptable as an agricultural reference. However, *we're going to grow our business* (or *profits* or *market share*) is incorrect usage. *We want to increase our business* is a much better choice, not only because it's more graceful, but also because it's easy to attach a percentage of growth to this statement. *Our goal is to grow our business 20 percent* is awkward and imprecise, but *we hope to increase our sales by 20 percent* is concrete and understandable. In some circumstances, *build* is a useful alternative to *grow*.

A second intransitive verb that seems to have taken on an unpleasant transitive form is *to migrate*. Today it's not unusual to hear *we migrated the programs to the new platform*. In fact, we may have moved them, but we did not migrate them, because things cannot be migrated. They migrate; that is, they move from place to place by themselves. *Move, relocate,* or *transfer* are good replacements for this improper use of *migrate.*

THE *-IZE* HAVE IT: CINDERELLA AND AT LEAST ONE UGLY STEPSISTER

In business English today, there's usually a serviceable word that has been corrupted by adding *-ize* or sometimes *-ization*. This suffix, which is unnecessary, makes the word atrocious as well as harder to pronounce. See the following list for several examples.

Ugly Stepsister	*Cinderella*
Absolutize	Create an absolute
Annuitize	Buy or receive an annuity
Anonymize	Make anonymous
Apostrophize	Add an apostrophe
Bucketize/Siloize	Classify, sort
Bulletize	Create a bulleted list
Calendarize	Schedule, to break into equal blocks of time
Commoditize	Turn a once-unique product into an inexpensive, undifferentiated commodity
Componentize	Break into parts
Concretize	Specify, define
Conversationalize	Simplify language
Disambiguize	Clarify
Disincentivize	Discourage
Finalize	Complete
Genericize	Become so well known that your brand name stands for an entire class or products, e.g., Kleenex (alternatively, make something, such as a speech, applicable to different audiences)
Hispanicize/Asianize	Make an environment more friendly for Spanish-speaking/Asian customers

Hysterectomize, vasectomize	Perform a hysterectomy, vasectomy
Incentivize	Offer rewards
Logoize	Add a logo
Modualize	Create a training module
Musicalize	Set to music
Narcotize	Administer a narcotic
Operationalize	Put into practice
Parameterize	Set boundaries
Partisanize	Take a political stance
Potentialize	Seek greatest potential
Reverbiagize	Reword, rewrite
Templatize	Create a template
Zeroize	Reset

Financial services representatives (formerly called bankers) are fond of a particularly obscure word: *monetize*. This word has actual meanings, which are "to establish as legal tender" and "to coin money." However, that's not what bankers mean when they talk about "monetizing strategies." What they do mean is anyone's guess, and if I had a banker who talked that way, I'd find one who was more interested in communicating with me than in trying to impress me with hollow terminology that even she doesn't understand.

Unfortunately, other industries have seized on *monetize* and the word has been corrupted to mean "to make money on every transaction." Why not just say that?

EUPHEMISMS: NOT JUST ANOTHER PRETTY FACE

A euphemism is the substitution of an inoffensive word or phrase for one that may be embarrassingly direct. Euphemisms rise in response to taboos—the things people feel uncomfortable talking about in polite conversation. Taboo subjects may include death, bodily functions, illness, loss, and sex.

Surprisingly, the three things your mother told you never

to talk about—money, religion, and politics—aren't really taboos, and there aren't as many euphemisms in these realms as there are in the others, unless you count *conservative* as a euphemism for "blood-sucking, profit-crazed, Bible-spouting fascist" or *liberal* for "tax-and-spend, bleeding-heart, godless, baby-killing Communist."

Euphemisms are not intrinsically evil; they are meant to make discourse about touchy subjects palatable. However, euphemisms cause damage when they are used to convince people that actions such as firing hundreds of employees, stealing, committing fraud, or violating the laws of civilized society are neutral or even harmless. In these cases, calling upon euphemisms is a strategy for avoiding responsibility and ducking consequences. Substituting the word *device* for *bomb* makes it seem as if a nuclear weapon is no more lethal than a can opener. That's linguistically slippery and dishonest.

The following list contains some euphemisms that conceal the truth and should be avoided.

The Spineless Euphemism	*The Real Word*
Adjusted the workforce, dehired, deselected, downsized, outplaced, reduced in force, reduced the census, rightsized, shortened the path to profitability, terminated, involuntary employee attrition, negative employee retention	Fired/Firing
Anger management issue	Hot temper
Bookkeeping irregularities	Fraud
Challenge, concern, issue	Problem
Collateral damage	Dead civilians
Compensated endorser	Paid spokesperson
Courtesy call	Telephone solicitation
Differently abled person	Person with a disability

Displaced inventory	Stolen property
Experiencing negative cash flow	Losing money
Final expenses	Funeral costs
Gaming (the word is acceptable if one means the *games industry*, especially games developed for computers)	Gambling
Gratitude	Bribe
Had a negative therapeutic outcome, in a condition incompatible with life	Died, dying
Healthy forests	Forests where logging is encouraged
High-yield bonds	Junk bonds
Intelligence gathering	Invasion
Intervention	Layoff
Involuntary separation, furlough	Spying
Loss prevention specialists	Store security guards
Member	Employee
Negative gain	Loss
Nonperforming asset	Bad loan
On hiatus	Canceled
Outage	Power failure
Person of interest	Suspect
Preowned	Used
Restructuring	Selling unprofitable divisions and firing people
Reutilization marketing facility	Junkyard
Revenue enhancement	Tax increase
Revenue shortfall	Debt
Sharpshooter	Sniper
Shrinkage	Theft
Studio apartment	One-room apartment
Substance abuse, novelty-seeking behavior	Addiction
Trade safeguard	Tariff
Transfer tube	Body bag

Undocumented worker, visitor	Illegal alien
Upscale	Rich
Vertically challenged	Short

WHAT? WHAT? ONE HUNDRED (OR SO) COMMON REDUNDANCIES

Redundancies aren't fatal; they're just annoying. Pruning your oral inventory cleans up your speech and makes it more forthright and artful. The list below gives some prime examples of redundancies to eliminate.

ACT (American College Test) test
Added bonus (or even worse, *extra added bonus*)
Advance planning/reservations
All-inclusive
AM in the morning, PM in the afternoon or evening
And plus
ATM (automatic teller machine) machine
Basic essentials/fundamentals
Big/small in size
Biography of his/her life
Blend/combine/mix together
But however
Categorically deny
Center median
Close proximity
Commute back and forth/in and out
Complete and total
Complete destruction

Convicted felon
Cooperate together
Customary/usual tradition
Definite decision
DVD (digital video disc) disc
Early pioneer
Empty space
End result
Equal halves
Exact same
Final conclusion/outcome/result
Final destination
Foot pedal
Foreign imports
Free gift
General consensus (of opinion)
General public
Great big
HIV (human immunodeficiency virus) virus
Honest truth
Hot water heater

Initially introduced
Inner feelings
Innocent bystander
IRA (Individual Retirement Account) account
Jewish rabbi
Join together
Knots per hour (a knot is one nautical mile per hour, so although miles per hour is acceptable, knots per hour is not; you'll need this one when you go yachting with the boss)
LCD (liquid crystal display) display
Little tiny
Meet together
Never at any time
New beginning
New construction
New discovery/innovation
Old cliché/proverb
Open forum
Passing fad
Past experience/history/memories
PCV (pollution control valve) valve
Personal friends
Personal opinion
PIN (personal identification number) number
Pizza pie

Popular favorite
Postpone until later
Present incumbent
RAM (random-access memory) memory/ROM (read-only memory) memory
Regular routine
Repeat again
Rise up
Rough estimate
RPMs (revolutions per minute) per minute
Safe haven
SAT (Scholastic Aptitude Test) test
Separate entities
Serious crisis
Soup du jour of the day
Specific details/example
Split apart
Sum total
Surrounded on all sides
Sworn affidavit
True facts
VIN (vehicle identification number) number
Visible to the eye
Tuna fish
Unexpected surprise
Unintentional error
Unique individual
UPC (Universal Product Code) code

TWO FOR THE PRICE OF ONE

A subset of redundancy consists of doublets: two words that are similar or identical in meaning and are linked by a conjunction such as *and* or *or*. Since they're nothing more than aural wallpaper, you should avoid using the following expressions:

Cease and desist (unless you're a lawyer writing a specific type of order)

Cool and calm (or its triplet version: calm, cool, and collected)

Each and every

Few and far between

First and foremost

Hale and hearty

Pick and choose

Safe and sound

Tried and true

AND FOR OUR LAST TRICK, THE DISAPPEARING CLICHÉ!

Closely allied with redundancies are clichés—those banal, overworked expressions that take the place of vigorous, original speech and bore your listeners. You'll want to jettison these:

Been there, done that (bought the T-shirt)

Benchmarking

Bottom line

Continuous improvement

Deploy

Diversity (It beats *integration*, but *inclusivity* says it better)

Exceed expectations

Global

Good news . . . bad news

Heavy hitter

Lean and mean

Level the playing field

Move the cheese (or my cheese)

Net-net

New and improved (An old product may be improved, but that doesn't make it new)

No-brainer

On the same page

Partnering

Rocket science, brain surgery, or rocket surgery

Service provider (Doctors, nurses, pharmacists, technicians, or even prostitutes, who by the way, are now called *sex workers*)

Sing from the same hymn-book

Slice and dice

Takeaway/take home

Take no prisoners

Take to the next level

Talk the talk

Team player

User-friendly

Viable option

Walk the walk

Window of opportunity

You go, girl

Zero-sum game

Is there anything left to say after you've removed so much from your vocabulary? Plenty. And speaking plain English endears you to your listeners and immediately makes what you say more potent and memorable.

I REALLY WANT THE JOB

SOUNDING SMART IN INTERVIEWS

TAKING THE COLD OUT OF THE CALL

An interview for a job can begin almost anywhere—even in a coffee shop or at a party—but often an interview starts with a cold call. You're looking for work and you start phoning businesses you think might be hiring. Although you may view this activity as simply information-gathering, the minute the person on the other end picks up the phone, it's an interview, and you have to think of it that way. You're selling yourself, and you're doing it by your words and manner alone.

On the telephone, there's no such thing as nonverbal communication. There are no facial expressions to moderate what you say. Telephone interactions are all about words and the tone of voice used to convey them, so if you're going to look for a job using the phone, your oral presentation skills should be top drawer.

Here's a type of call many businesses receive every day, and I can guarantee that 99.99 percent of these calls garner a negative response: "Hi, I'm a recent graduate, and I'm calling to find out if you guys have any openings."

When I receive an unsolicited call like this—and I often do because my business is located in a city with a large university— I may take some time with the caller, explaining that I don't have a position to offer, but I do have a bit of advice. If the caller is receptive, I share the following tips for cold calling.

Learn about the business and the person you're calling. Remember those nouns that have become verbs? One of them is *to google*, even though the company is sensitive about this nearly ubiquitous use of its trademarked name. If you have access to the Web, look up the person and company you're phoning. Google is a fountain of information and, by reading just a few citations, you can learn a lot about the company's focus and latest projects.

For example, suppose you want a job writing technical documentation. You start researching companies that provide writing services and find a small firm called ABC Editorial. By taking a minute or two to research the company, you discover that it specializes in medical, financial, educational, and nonprofit communications. There's no mention of technology clients, which probably means the firm isn't a prime target for you. You can eliminate it from your list, saving you the trouble of calling and the company representative the time it takes to answer the phone.

Identify yourself. When someone answers the phone, tell the person who you are, using both your first and last names. "Hi" is not a sufficient salutation for a business call. Ask for the person whose name you've researched or for her department—or for the department where you'd like to work.

Speak distinctly. The telephone amplifies mush-mouth tendencies; if the listener can't see you, she doesn't have the visual cues she needs to interpret what you're saying, and she can't read your lips to fill in what she doesn't hear. If you're Bob Robertson, but you pronounce it "Buh Robisuh," either because your speech is lazy or you're in too much of a hurry to enunciate, the listener still doesn't know who you are and probably isn't inclined to ask you to repeat your name.

Don't say "you guys." Probably half the people you'll be talking to will be women. Either *you* or *your company* stands in for this tactless and far too casual expression.

Speak pleasantly and with enthusiasm. If you sound bored or as if you're reading a script, you won't impress anyone. Even on the telephone, a smile works, and a positive attitude is contagious.

Add some qualifications. Did you major in agricultural management or theater or journalism? What sort of position are you looking for? Do you want to write brochures and reports, create public relations campaigns, or be an administrative assistant? The person you're talking with might have nothing available, but if she knows a bit about your background, perhaps she might be able to refer you to someone else. If you're not a new graduate, tell her something about your recent work experience and your career interests.

Make your pitch succinct and relevant. Boil down your reasons for calling into a very few clear, positive sentences, and deliver them with warmth and zest.

Practice your pitch. You don't want to sound rehearsed, but you do want to get your best features on the table. Writing and practicing key points will help you remember what you want to include and ensure that you come across as a serious professional, not a frat boy or a valley girl.

Say thank you. No one gets a job offer on the basis of one cold call, but the information you received by calling was valuable—even if all you learned was that the company wasn't hiring—and the person on the phone spent time with you. That's worth a thank-you. One young person I heard about went so far as to send a thank-you note to the receptionist who took his call, acknowledging her kindness in speaking with him. That single act of courtesy made him stand out, and she referred him to several people within the company. A few weeks later, an entry-level job opened up, and she called to give him a heads-up. Guess who jumped to the front of the line and landed the job?

If you reach voice mail instead of a person, the same rules

apply. Because many companies send all incoming calls to voice mail, it's a good idea to practice a pitch that takes no more than twenty seconds to deliver. Your message should be professional, enthusiastic, and, above all, concise.

> Good morning, this is Bob Robertson. I'm a recent *summa cum laude* graduate of Big University, and I'm looking for a position writing technical documentation. I worked part-time with X Corp while I was in school, and now I'd like to enter the field full-time. My number is (310) 555-5555. If you have a position I could apply for, I hope you'll return my call. Once again, that's Bob Robertson at (310) 555-5555. Thank you.

Quick Tip: A Word to Young Interviewees

Your first "real" job interview may occur while you're in college, and college slang is ubiquitous, most of it having to do with sex, drugs, drinking, and the aftermath of sex, drugs, and drinking. While you're in the dorm, there's no reason to avoid the slang that makes you part of the community.

However, the moment you step into the world of work, whether you're at an on-campus recruitment event or a work-site interview, leave college-speak behind. Customers, clients, and coworkers will come from all walks of life, and you must speak appropriately and professionally with everyone you encounter. During the interview process and throughout your early career you need to avoid expressions such as:

All about ("I'm all about people and customer service")
All over ("I'll be all over making your business a success")
All up in ("I'll be all up in your face trying to learn everything I can")
Awesome ("Your company mission is awesome")
Bogus ("I think your competition's claims are bogus")
Down with ("I'm totally down with your goals")

Because your voice mail is the telephonic equivalent of an unsolicited résumé, the chances of a return call from a message like this are slim, but you'll increase even those odds if your message is well crafted and carefully delivered.

THE FRIEND-OF-A-FRIEND CALL

Sometimes your call is one step up the ladder from being a cold call. You've done your research and discovered you know someone at the company, and that person has said you may use his name when you call. Although your inside contact is helpful, it's not all there is to getting in the door: you still must prepare a careful, succinct pitch.

Duh ("Did I research your company? Duh")

Get behind ("I can get behind your growth plans")

Off the hook ("My communication style is very upbeat, totally off the hook")

Sweet ("Your last campaign was off-the-hook sweet")

Totally ("I totally understand what you're getting at")

Uber- anything ("Your business objectives are ubersmart")

Way anything ("I'm way more qualified than your other candidates")

What's up with that? ("I read your financial reports and saw you had negative cash flow. What's up with that?")

The examples above are simply overused and annoying. However, some slang expressions are truly disgusting and have no place—ever—in business conversation. Also, please remember that there are some words that have entered the common parlance of youth that are still beyond the pale in the business setting. Avoid phrases such as *That sucks* (or *that blows*) or utterances that include *ass*, *bitch*, *butt*, *crap*, and *fart*. Although they sound innocent to you, they may offend your interviewer.

Generally, your inside contact has given you the name of the person to talk to, so make sure to use it. "Good morning, Ms. Taylor. This is Bob Robertson, and Jake Williams suggested I get in touch with you." (If Jake is well known within the company, you won't have to tell Ms. Taylor who he is, but if he toils in relative obscurity, you might mention the department where he works.) "I'm a recent *summa cum laude* graduate of Big University with a degree in technical communications. I've been working part-time while completing my coursework, but I'm looking for a full-time position. Jake said you were the person I should talk with about possible employment with your firm."

If she says there are no openings, you might ask if you could come in to meet with her for a brief informational interview. If she agrees to that and you make a good impression on her during the meeting, she will probably remember you when an opening occurs.

If Ms. Taylor really isn't the person to talk with, she still may be a conduit to someone else. If she directs you to another person or department, thank her and call the person she suggests, who may be in Human Resources—which is often a black hole. If you're lucky, however, she'll send you right to the person who handles the firm's technical communication.

You now have two names to use with the next person in line. "Good morning, Mr. Higgins. Jake Williams and Ellen Taylor both suggested I get in touch with you." Then make your pitch and see what happens. You may be told there's nothing available, or you may be asked to fill out an application online or in person.

Again, if Mr. Higgins says there are no openings, try to arrange an informational interview; a good interview can make you memorable the next time a position is available.

Unless your contact is the president of the company who also happens to be your father or mother, don't assume that having an inside source guarantees you a job. All it does—perhaps—is make the person on the other end of the line a little more helpful. Watch your tone of voice and don't be cocky. Confidence is an asset, but arrogance will undo all the good your inside contact provides. *Please* and *thank you* get you much further than egotism will.

GETTING PAST THE GATEKEEPER

The vast majority of decision makers screen their calls, and they often position their administrative assistants as guardians of the gate. Even if you're doing the friend-of-a-friend call, Ms. Taylor may very well be inaccessible to you. In that case, you might ask your friend if he would intercede and make an introduction for you, just to say that you'll be calling. That way, Ms. Taylor can tell her assistant to put you through. If your friend is willing to make such a call for you, show initiative by following up right away. The assistant won't remember your name forever.

Some decision makers come into the office early or stay late. Most of them do so to get some quiet work done before the pace of the day speeds up or after everyone's gone home, and they usually don't answer their phones during these periods. It's worth a try, though. The person you want to speak with might pick up—but don't waste her time. State your purpose, listen carefully to the response, thank her, and end the call.

No matter how careful your preparations, some gate-keepers are very tough cookies. If you aren't on her boss's "put them through anytime" list, you don't get through. In that case, ask for the decision maker's voice mail or e-mail address. If the assistant won't give those up, then make your pitch to her directly and ask for her e-mail address. In your follow-up e-mail to her, mention that it was pleasant to speak with her (even if it was worse than a root canal), repeat your pitch in written form—and hope it moves up the chain. Don't ever disrespect the assistant; speaking with her in a professional, congenial manner may disarm her to the point that she eventually lets you speak with her boss.

GETTING WARMER

Suppose you're beyond the cold-call stage. You've sent a résumé, and the company has jumped on it. Someone from Human Resources calls. Once again, although you may not realize it, your interview has begun. How you handle the phone conversation may be entered into a file or at least informally noted.

If the caller asks for you, the proper response is "This is she" or "This is he," not "This is her," "This is him," or the even less-professional "This is" or "Yeah." "Speaking" is okay, but it sometimes sounds a little pompous—and pomposity is something you want to avoid. Next, you and the caller negotiate a time for your interview. Before you hang up, be sure to mention that you're looking forward to the meeting and thank the caller. By doing so, you sound gracious and well mannered, and both qualities are appreciated.

THE PHONE TAG INTERVIEW

Should you not be available when the call comes from a recruiter or interviewer, what will that person hear on your voice mail? Cutesy greetings featuring your dog or your two-year-old child are fine for friends, but those messages should be deep-sixed when you're expecting an important business call.

A good outgoing voice mail message should include these elements:

- Your name
- A request for a message from the other person
- A time frame in which he or she can expect to hear back from you

Don't make your outgoing voice mail greeting so long that callers have to wait forever to leave their message, and there's no reason to fall back on the standard message about being on the phone or away from the desk. Callers really don't care where you are. Once they've found out you're not picking up, they want to get on with their part of the exchange.

Some people change their greeting every day or every week, which is a great idea if you keep your recordings current. However, it's disconcerting to hear, "It's Thursday, November 2," when it's really Wednesday, November 8.

Make sure your tone is professional but welcoming. The following are some examples of excellent voice mail.

For an office with no administrative support. "Hello, this is Samantha Smith. I'm sorry I'm not available to take your call right now. At the tone, please leave a message of any length, including the best time for me to reach you. I'll call you back promptly, and I look forward to speaking with you soon. Goodbye."

A daily updated message. "Hello, this is Jack Jones at Amalgamated Ant Farms. Today is Monday, October 26, and I'm in the office all day. Please leave your message at the tone, and I'll return your call today."

A weekly updated message. "Hello, this is Grace Gladman. Today is Monday, October 26. I'm in the office today, but I'll be away Tuesday and Wednesday. On Thursday I'll be available only from 2 PM to 4 PM. I'll be in all day Friday. I check my voice mail frequently, so if you'll leave your message at the tone, I'll return your call as soon as possible."

AND AT THE OTHER END

You're interested in the interview, and you call the recruiter back. Now she isn't available, so it's your turn to leave a voice mail message. Do a sloppy job of it and you may find that you've thrown a stumbling block in your own path. Here's what *not* to say:

> Hi, Ms. Richards. I'm sorry I missed your call. My dog got sick and I had to take him to the vet. I thought I was going to have to put him down, but he's doing

better, thank goodness. Anyway, I'd love to talk with
you about the job. Please call me at (614) 555-5555.
I'm here most of the time, and if you don't reach me,
I guess we'll just keep trying till we get it right. Thanks
a lot for calling me. I hope to speak with you soon.

This message doesn't work for many reasons. First of all,
Ms. Richards doesn't need to know why she couldn't reach
you. You weren't there—end of story. Second, she may be
calling many candidates for many positions and your message
is so vague she may not remember which one you're calling
about. Third, your breezy attitude about making connections
is neither charming nor witty; it's disrespectful because it
sounds as if you couldn't care less about when—or even if—
you talk with her. Last, if she didn't write your phone number
down when you gave it the first time, she'll have to go back
through your whole meandering message again to find it.

Your unprofessional approach to this important message
may destroy your chances for an interview; Ms. Richards has
the option of not returning your call, and given your telephone
performance, it's likely she'll decide not to, especially if she's
already spoken with or listened to voice mail messages from
candidates who sound more promising than you do.

Your return voice mail message, which should not exceed
twenty seconds, should include these four elements:

- Your name
- The reason for your call
- How and when the recruiter can reach you
- Another iteration of your phone number and a graceful
  close

When the beep sounds, you're on stage. Make your
entrance and lines memorable. If you think you'll forget something important, write your message down before you call and
refer to it as you speak.

Good morning, Ms. Richards. This is Catherine Kumar. I'm returning your call about interviewing for the copywriting position in your corporate communications department. I'm in a meeting most of the day today, but I'm available all day tomorrow at (614) 555-5555. I look forward to hearing from you then. Once again, this is Catherine Kumar at (614) 555-5555. Thank you.

You'll notice that Catherine repeats her phone number at the end of the call. The repetition should be slow and distinct. Too often, callers blurt out their return numbers very quickly, making it difficult for the other person to understand them and return the call. But if you follow the script just provided, you'll likely be on your way to an interview.

THE UNEXPECTED INTERVIEW

You and Ms. Richards have finally made contact. You thought she'd be setting up a time for you to come in for an interview, but she says she'd rather do an initial screening on the phone.

Some interviewers prefer to catch candidates on the fly to see how well they do on the spur of the moment; others like the job seeker to be comfortable and prepared. If you feel you aren't ready to make your best impression, you can always try to schedule a different time for the "discussion." Express genuine regret and have a plausible, business-related excuse for being unavailable. You're going into a meeting in five minutes, or you must leave immediately for an appointment across town, but you'd be happy to call the interviewer back later in the day or even tomorrow at her convenience. That's reasonable, and it gives you at least an hour or two to down a cappuccino and prepare.

In fact, you already should be thoroughly prepared. More and more companies are relying on the telephone screening interview. Their goal is to save money by separating the "possibles" from the "probables." Your goal is to use this initial interview as a springboard to an in-house meeting. You must be as prepared for this on-the-spot interview as you would be for a face-to-face session. If you aren't ready, you'd better get ready now.

Although some telephone interviews are as short as ten minutes and consist of no more than a few questions about the details of your résumé or clarification about your previous employment, the session may last as long as an hour and delve into specifics about how you have handled or would deal with various scenarios. Since you don't know how the interview will be structured, you have to be prepared for anything.

A recently laid-off aerospace engineer I spoke with says,

> I've done twelve one-hour phone interviews, mostly within my own company, in the last nine days. Some of them are right off the shelf. The interviewer is clearly asking the same questions of everyone. I understand the reason for that; he's trying to give everyone an equal chance, and he thinks the only way to do that is to ask identical questions. It's dull, though.
>
> The other interviews have been far more interesting because I got to talk about my experience inside the company and how what I've done in one division translates to another. That's an advantage because I haven't had to do a lot of formal research. I've been with the company for twenty years already, and I know the way it functions. I'm now closing in on a new job and think it will be offered in the next few days.

PREPPING FOR SUCCESS

Unless you're like the engineer, interviewing within your own corporation, interview preparation involves extensive research and hours of practice. You must first ferret out as much detail about the company as you can. The bare minimum you should do is to read every page of the company Web site and annual report.

Scan the local paper for relevant news items or enlist a search engine that will undoubtedly dump far too many citations into your lap. Cull through them and create your own profile of the company—its long-term successes, short-term problems, status among its peers, and every other salient point you can find.

But don't stop there. The company doesn't exist in a vacuum. Go to the library or hop online to read some journals related to the industry. Look for trends and issues of concern. How is the industry being affected by changes in technology, the economy, and the regulatory climate? Is the chairperson or CEO featured prominently in any of the articles you unearth? What are her perspectives on the industry and the business climate in general?

Quiz people you know inside the organization. Peruse the names of the board of directors, advisory board, and officers to see if you're acquainted with anyone in a position of authority. If Uncle Bob or Aunt Grace is a member of the in group, or you know someone who knows someone, get to him as quickly as possible and ask for any nonproprietary information he can give you.

All these bits of data will make it easier for you to speak confidently and without hesitation when you interview. You can work your company knowledge into the conversation subtly as you highlight your own experience and skills.

While you're researching the company, interview yourself as well. What are your successes that you want to put in the spotlight during the interview? If you're a recent graduate, were you a member of student government? Did you earn scholastic honors? Serve as a departmental fellow or assistant to a professor? Have you participated in research projects or completed several internships in your field? Were they substantive experiences that give you an edge over other candidates?

If you've been working for a while, what are your most relevant and outstanding skills? What are your most outstanding accomplishments? Have you increased sales or profits? Have you developed successful products or led teams?

What are your long-term personal and professional goals? Where do you want to live? What best exemplifies your style of management? What kind of supervision do you prefer? Knowing your strengths and greatest successes makes it easier for you to plan your answers to the questions you should expect from an interviewer.

ON THE PHONE

The advantage of a telephone interview is that the interviewer can't see you. You can surround yourself with cheat sheets: your résumé and cover letter; your extensive research about the company; salary surveys for the type of job under discussion; some well-thought-out answers to typical interview questions; a short roster of accomplishments that are germane to the job you're seeking; and, very important, a list of questions about the position. Interviewers always want to know if you have questions; if you don't, you sound uninterested at best and dumbfounded at worst.

As you interview, be sure not to rustle all that paper. Spread everything out on the desk or tape it up on the wall so it's visible at a glance.

Although the interviewer can't see all your preparations, she can hear a great deal, so no gum chewing, eating, or drinking while you're interviewing. You may want to keep a glass of water handy for wetting your lips, but don't gulp. Take a bathroom break before the interview.

Turn off any distracting noise: television, radio, computers that chime when you receive a message. If you're interviewing from home, foist the kids and animals off on a friend for a couple of hours. Close the door to the area you're calling from. Turn off call waiting. You don't need a series of beeps interrupting the flow of your conversation.

When it comes to the interview itself, be sure you obtain the name, phone number, and address of the person handling the interview because you'll want to hand-write a brief thank-you note after your time together. Once the housekeeping details are out of the way, the most important thing you can do is to listen carefully to each question. Make sure the interviewer has finished speaking before you jump into the conversation. If you need time to consider your answer, say so. However, too long a pause without explanation may make the interviewer think you've fallen asleep or gone off to make a sandwich.

Yes and no responses shut down conversation and sound curt and unfriendly, so amplify your answers purposefully, connecting the substance of the question to your qualifications and experience. Smile when appropriate; it will make you sound approachable, even if you're nervous.

Some experts recommend that you stand up for the entire interview, because it brings more life to your voice. If you're comfortable moving around while you speak and you can see your notes while you're on your feet, it's an idea you might consider.

Refer to your notes to make your answers accurate and precise. As the interview nears its end, ask one or two of your prepared questions, and thank the interviewer for her time.

Don't be shy about indicating your interest in the job. I once sat on a panel of interviewers who talked with thirteen applicants over a period of five days. Of all the candidates, only one said specifically that the job sounded exactly like what she was looking for and that she hoped we would invite her for a formal interview. As the committee moved toward a selection, she was one of two finalists. She once again emphasized her interest. That enthusiasm made the difference between her and the other candidate. She got the job, turned a troubled organization around, and brilliantly vindicated the hiring committee's choice.

It's permissible to ask the interviewer when you should expect to hear back from her. You might not get a definite answer, because the hiring process teems with variables, but the interviewer should at least be able to estimate a time frame.

OFF THE PHONE AND INTO THE OFFICE

You made it through the screening and are one of a few candidates coming in for a face-to-face interview. There are many books and Web sites that deal with interview preparation, and some of them are exceptionally helpful. These resources have useful tips and hints about dress, decorum, and even what to eat if a meal is part of your interview process; most of them also provide extensive lists of interview questions and suggested answers. However, be leery about adopting any canned responses to interview questions. Although the books and Web sites contain the types of questions you'll probably hear in your interview, take the time to craft your own unique responses. Experienced interviewers have read the books and visited the Web sites, too, and they can spot a rote answer a mile away. Here are a few of the comprehensive Web sites—those that offer salary information, insider tips, research, résumé help, and other topics:

- www.knockemdead.com
- www.wetfeet.com
- www.vault.com

If you rely on a published list and memorize what appears to be a good response to a specific question, you may be totally unprepared for follow-up questions, and any interviewer who's listening carefully to what you say will have follow-ups. You run the risk of whipsawing between being brilliant and articulate at one minute and grasping for the right words the next. So extensive preparation is in, but memorizing is out.

One essential aspect of preparation is practice. Write down some potential questions and rehearse your answers. Gather a group of friends and colleagues who've been through the interview process several times. Have them stand in for your interviewer, ask tough questions, and critique your responses and your way of presenting yourself. Instruct them to be brutal in their evaluation. The only way to improve your technique is through honest feedback.

There are literally thousands of questions someone can ask you in an interview. You cannot fashion an answer for every one, but if you read the questions you'll find on Web sites or in the interview books, you'll discern patterns and be able to prepare more extensively than you might believe. Crafting a good answer to any of the general questions in each category provides a good start for answering all of them.

These patterns include questions about your personal strengths (and weaknesses), experience, work habits, future plans and goals, interpersonal skills, potential for success within this particular company, management style (if applicable), and salary expectations.

THE INTERVIEW

The function of an interview is simply to see if you are a good match for a given job. It is not a one-way transaction in which you sit with flop sweat running down your back, trying to dredge up what you think the interviewer wants to hear. An interview is a conversation between or among reasonable adults. There's never any need to panic. The worst that can happen is that this opportunity doesn't work for you. Remember that you're sizing up the company as much as its representatives are assessing you.

Is the company a good fit for your own needs? Is the interview an exercise in intimidation or an opportunity for meaningful exchange? It's normal to have a few butterflies, but an air of unruffled self-confidence is attractive to interviewers (and that confidence comes from extensive preparation and practice).

As you enter the office, be polite and pleasant to the receptionist. Address her by name; she may be asked to share her first impressions of you with the interview team. Present your card and say you have an appointment with the interviewer.

While you wait, extend your antennae. Look around. What's on the walls? Generic artwork? Awards and honors? What kinds of furnishings do you see? Plastic chairs that look as if they belong in a bus station or comfortable seating and attractive lighting? What magazines are displayed, or are there other types of reading materials? Is the receptionist sitting behind bulletproof glass, in a cubicle, or in the middle of the room?

Do you hear music? Is it Bach or Eminem? As people move in and out of the reception area, what are they wearing? Do they smile and seem welcoming or are they pale, hunched, and preoccupied? All these sensory cues tell you something about the culture of the company, and they also give you topics for a moment of small talk with the interviewer before you get down to business.

I once interviewed a man who had read the company's mission statement, which was prominently displayed in the elevator, on the way to the interview. It was a new statement, so I knew he hadn't seen it in our literature yet. He had obviously studied it as he rode up to my office. During the interview, he referred to it a couple of times and mentioned how his personal beliefs dovetailed with our goals. It was an impressive performance. After several more meetings, he got the job. Observing the details can make the difference between you and a candidate who shows no interest in the environment.

As the interview begins, remember to speak clearly and simply. Avoid jargon and industry buzzwords, even if your interviewer uses them extensively. Moderate your tone and your pace; don't yell or whisper, and don't race through your answers.

Some interviews for high-level positions may actually involve your solving a problem or working together with other candidates. However, the decision to pass you on for further consideration is made at the first interview. The questions you can be almost certain will arise include:

Tell me about yourself. Resist the temptation to chronicle your life beginning with the day of your birth. The interviewer really doesn't want to hear much about you except as it relates to the job. So it's best to begin with your educational background (don't start with elementary school); add some career highlights, and end with your interest in learning more about the position.

Why are you leaving your current position? Even if you're leaving because the boss can't keep his hands to himself or you're locked into a dead-end situation, there's no need to dwell on the negative. Most people change jobs because they're looking for an opportunity to advance and further their careers; those reasons are certainly acceptable. If there are further dimensions you want to explore in your answer, you're free to do so. Just keep your answers positive. If you speak ill of your current boss, the interviewer may assume you won't be any more loyal to your next boss. And disloyalty is often the kiss of death.

Were you fired? If the interviewer is asking the question, he probably knows the answer and is looking for honesty. Today, there are myriad reasons for being let go: mergers, branch office closures, company bankruptcy, or sending work out of the country. There's no shame in confessing that you were one of five thousand people who lost their jobs in a massive layoff.

Tell me about your experience. If you're a recent graduate, discuss any relevant coursework, internships, or part-time jobs you've held. If your previous experience is unrelated to your current job search, emphasize your responsibilities and how you fulfilled them.

What are your personal and professional goals for the next five years? The purpose of this question is to probe for commitment and ambition. Do you see yourself with this company in five years? It costs time and money to train someone; it may be as much as a year or more before a new hire really knows his way around the culture and begins to make meaningful contributions. If you're a job-hopper, you'll waste a great deal of the company's resources. "I go where the wind takes me" is not the way to answer this question. And if you're interviewing with your potential boss, "I want to be sitting in your chair" isn't smart either. It's possible she wants to be sitting there in five years, too, and this answer can sound more ruthless than ambitious.

Why are you better for this job than other candidates we're interviewing? This question uncovers arrogance as opposed to self-assurance. Be gracious and don't run down the other candidates; they obviously have similar qualifications or they wouldn't have been invited to interview. This is the time to stress *your* experience, *your* skills, and *your* successes. If you have one or two overwhelming qualifications, such as a strong work ethic and demonstrated results, sell those, but not by disparaging others who are also swimming in the interview pool.

What are your strengths and weaknesses? In answering this question, it's best not to babble on and on about your brilliance. Pick two or three qualities that will be necessary in the new position and stress how you've found that those qualities have contributed to your prior success. When it comes to your weaknesses, one is enough, and once again tie it to the job. Be certain that management could view this "weakness" as a positive. For example, "I press hard to complete assignments on deadline, and I can get impatient if other people's commitment to projects is not as intense." You can also spotlight something you've decided to work on that will be useful now and in the future. "Since the country is rapidly moving toward being bilingual, I'm updating my skills in Spanish. I'm taking a conversational Spanish course, and I also have a taped course I use in the car."

Why do you want to work here? Don't say that you've heard they have high salaries and great benefits. This question is not about what you expect to get, but what you hope to give to the organization. It's the big opportunity to showcase your research. Pick one or two things that impressed you as you studied the company, and show how your skills and talents mesh with the company's initiatives and culture.

What salary do you expect? "All the money you ever thought of" may be the truth, but it's not the best answer. Do your homework. Research salary surveys, visit industry Web sites that offer pay information, and ask friends who hold similar jobs what you might expect. At this early stage, you don't want to name a figure so high you price yourself out of the job or so low you peg yourself as desperate. Say that you need to know more about the job before you can come to a decision about that question. Mention that while salary is obviously important, the complete compensation package is also of interest to you, so you can't name a specific figure until you've had more discussion.

If the interviewer presses, lean on your research, indicate that salary is negotiable. If he continues to push for an answer, you can say, "According to the industry sources, the range for this type of position in this market is between X and Y. Because I have ten years' experience in the industry, I'd expect to begin near the top of that range." If you're shorter on experience, you can turn that into a plus. "I'm well acquainted with the industry, but obviously there would be a learning curve for me with this company. I'd be willing to start in the middle of the range, but if I perform well, I'd want to increase my salary within a reasonable length of time."

You can turn the question around and ask for help from the interviewer. "I'm familiar with the various ranges in this market, but, of course, I don't know your exact pay scales. What do you typically offer for this kind of position? Are you competitive with the market?" Once the interviewer provides a figure, you know where to pitch your response.

In general, it's best not to discuss money until the job has been offered. At that point, you've proven yourself to the interview team and it's the right time for negotiation. When you're still an unknown quantity, too high a salary expectation too early in the process may become an excuse for showing you the door.

If the interviewer insists that you name a figure, you have no choice. Based on the results of your research, state a salary expectation.

When they've gathered all the general information they need, many interviewers move on to what are called behavioral questions, and there are literally thousands from which they can choose. You can spot these questions because they ask for specific information about how you have handled, or would handle, certain types of situations. "Tell me about . . ." is often a cue that a behavioral question is on the way.

The purpose of behavioral questions is to discover how you use the skills and abilities that are critical to job performance and how you interact with others. The interviewer is looking for concrete examples that showcase your abilities in important business functions such as building teams, dealing with difficult people, managing time, planning, balancing multiple priorities, budgeting, handling stress, and communicating. If you're new to the job market, you might hear questions such as:

- What did you most enjoy about college? What was the greatest challenge?
- What lessons did you learn from your best professor? What did you learn from the professor you liked least?
- Besides classes and work, what else did you do with your time on the campus?
- Did you learn more in class or outside the classroom?
- How many internships did you complete? Which one was most meaningful to you—and why?

More experienced candidates will not be asked about college, but you can expect these sorts of questions:

- How do you manage deadlines? Tell me about a time you missed a deadline. What were the consequences and what did you do about it?
- What would you do if you had approved a project that was going over budget?
- What's your preferred management style? Has it ever backfired? Tell me what you did about that.
- What type of supervision do you like? How do you work with a boss whose supervisory style differs from what you prefer?
- Has anyone ever claimed credit for one of your ideas? How did you deal with that?
- Tell me about a time you synthesized many opinions to arrive at a solution to a problem.
- Have you ever had to fire anyone? Tell me about that.

- Have you ever built a team from scratch? Tell me how you did it.
- Tell me about a time you were involved in a dispute with coworkers. How did you resolve the issue?
- If you have to discipline an employee, how do you do it?
- Can you work with little supervision? How do you motivate yourself to get the work done?

You can't wing behavioral questions, and that's why preparation is so critical. The interviewer will be looking for specific examples and personal anecdotes, so it's essential that you have those success stories burnished and at the ready.

Sometimes, out of nowhere will come a question that seems nonsensical, such as what animal you'd like to be or how you'd spend the perfect day. Obviously, these are psychological questions, probing for some underlying attitudes. A person who wants to be a squid is probably different from a person who wants to be an elephant, but if your entire interview comprises questions like this, you might think about looking for the door. Interviews should be about your skills, abilities, experience, education, and other measurable, relevant qualities. The interview process may include some psychological evaluation, but the initial meeting isn't the place for it.

You may also run into little horrors called brainteasers, pioneered at Microsoft and now used by many other companies. Designed to showcase creative thinking, these questions can be standard logic puzzles or more complicated questions, such as the title question of William Poundstone's book about brainteasers, *How Would You Move Mount Fuji?*[1] It's not as necessary to reach the right answer as it is to demonstrate how you'd tackle the problem. You're expected to think out loud and to share your thought processes with the interviewer.

These kinds of hypothetical questions can be fun, but only if you're prepared for the possibility that they might be asked. Otherwise, you can be caught off guard and end up slack-jawed with surprise. You'll find information about these questions at the Web sites mentioned earlier.

INTERVIEW CURVEBALL 1: THE MEAL INTERVIEW

Lunch or dinner interviews usually come late in the hiring process. No one's going to shell out for a meal unless you're being looked over seriously. However, the interview is not primarily about food and whether you know how to use the right fork. (You might want to brush up on etiquette, though. You don't want to come across as someone without manners.) The meal interview is more about behavior in a social setting, especially how you communicate, both verbally and nonverbally, in an out-of-office situation.

Although company representatives are eyeballing you, a meal interview is also a great opportunity for you to observe your host and any others who may have been invited. You'll get a real sense of the culture when everyone's at ease in a favorite watering hole. How they behave is as important as how you behave. When this interview is over, would you ever want to have another meal with these people?

The old rules about mealtime etiquette apply in these interviews: sit up straight, don't put your elbows on the table, don't talk with your mouth full, and don't wash down food with a beverage—all the things your mother told you. Don't order messy food, such as spaghetti or snails, that might skitter away or leave stains all over your shirt. Don't spark up a cigarette between courses, and for heaven's sake, don't order a cocktail, even if everyone else does. Alcohol does strange things to people who are already nervous, and you can't take the chance of slurring your words or saying something inappropriate. Your language skills are of paramount importance in any type of interview, so don't do anything that will impair your ability to speak intelligently and clearly.

What you have to say and how you speak to others will be watched closely. Interviewers are likely to be noting your interactions with servers, so it's essential that you speak courteously to wait staff. Say "please" rather than barking at them or ordering them around like your personal servants. Make eye contact and smile when you thank them for their service.

Turn off your cell phone before being seated. What could be more important than devoting your full attention to the interview? Taking calls at the table marks you as a rube, not a rising star.

Conversation during the meal may be more social than business-related, so be prepared with some small-talk topics and follow the lead of your host. Smiling and contributing to the conversation will stand you in good stead. It should go without saying—but unfortunately it can't—that swearing or telling racial or ethnic jokes cannot be part of the interview at any time, no matter what your tablemates do or say. They may be testing you.

When the "real" interview begins, either before or after the main portion of the meal, continue doing the things that got you there in the first place: listening, showing interest in the position, asking and answering questions, and enjoying the interchange.

There's no need for awkwardness when the check comes. If you're invited to a meal, the host pays, and you write a thank-you note.

INTERVIEW CURVEBALL 2:
THE PANEL INTERVIEW

After your screening interviews, you may be told you'll be meeting next with a panel. You'll probably be given a list of the panelists' names and titles, but if the list isn't forthcoming, ask for it. To do the best possible job, you have to know who's on the other side of the table and what perspectives they'll bring to the interview. Questions from a marketing representative may be very different from those of a financial officer.

In the words of Monty Python, "No one expects the Spanish Inquisition!" But the panel interview may feel like it. Remember, however, that just like any other interview, the panel interview is a two-way street; it's an opportunity to meet several company representatives at once, watch how they interact with one another, and decide if this is an atmosphere in which you're comfortable and can make a contribution. Listen and learn during this unique situation.

Although they usually are more formal and stiff than individual interviews, panel interviews can work in your favor. During a one-to-one interview, you have to impress one person, and if you don't scale the heights with that interviewer, your odds of getting the job are nil. However, if there are three people in the interview and you impress two of them, your chances of getting hired go up. If four interviewers out of five like your style, your odds jump again. Even if all the panelists don't carry equal weight in the hiring decision, the more of them you can impress, the better your prospects. And if you hit a home run with everyone, that's excellent indeed.

Because a panel interview is a time-saving measure, panelists are likely to ask the same questions of everyone. Panels try to ensure fairness, and the way to do that is to use a prepared script. However, it's not unusual for a panel to try to unnerve you a little, just to see how you do under pressure. Maintain your composure no matter what's thrown at you or how the panel behaves.

Although the interview may be conducted in rapid-fire fashion because the panelists have their questions down pat, don't be railroaded into rushing your answers. Take each question in turn, and try to answer it from the perspective of the questioner. Keep your answers as succinct as possible. The panel probably has to get through quite a roster of questions. Make it easy for them by being prepared to answer questions fully but concisely.

Listen carefully. You may pick up underlying themes you can address while you're dealing with the questions themselves. For example, several panelists may ask different questions that all refer in some way to various aspects of teamwork. Once you've identified that theme, you can spotlight your ability to work with teams in your answers to other questions.

You can say to the financial officer, "I consider the budget a critical part of any plan of action. When I led a cross-functional team through a complex marketing audit, we stayed under budget by 15 percent." You can answer a marketing question by saying, "As a team leader, it was my responsibility to assign roles, delegate, and follow up throughout the study. When the audit was complete, it had a significant impact on the way our company viewed the sales environment." These are good answers because they address both the technical aspects of the questions and the unspoken issue of teams.

Don't hesitate to ask your own questions. In the example above, if you pick up a theme, inquire about it. "I seem to be hearing that the organization relies a great deal on teamwork. Is that correct? How are teams selected and how do you judge the contributions of individual team members?" That should keep them busy for a while. Although you might not be able to ask questions within the context of the interview itself, most panels will give you a few minutes for follow-up questions before they dismiss you.

During the interview, your nonverbal skills are also on display. Eye contact with the panel is critical. Answer the questioner, but take stock of the entire panel as you speak. It's not only polite to do so, but you can also watch for body language that lets you know if you're on target. A nod is good; a glazed stare is not. See if there's anyone the rest of the panel defers to. They may look to him for approval of their questions or smile when he does. Although you cannot ignore the rest of the panel, be aware of the important role this person plays in the hiring decision and make sure he receives appropriate attention and eye contact.

As you leave, shake hands with all the members of the panel and thank them by name for taking the time to meet with you. If you know the job is not for you, that's all you need to do. However, if you're convinced that this is a good match, make eye contact and reiterate that you enjoyed the interview, you're still very interested in the job, and you hope they'll continue to consider you.

Write thank-you notes to each panel member. Although they interviewed you as a group, they are individual people, and they deserve individual attention. Also, writing to each one gives you an opportunity to comment on specific questions each person may have asked. It's a quick, easy, and impressive way to follow up. Even if you're going to withdraw your name from consideration, don't burn a bridge by being impolite; write the notes.

TO LAUGH OR NOT TO LAUGH: IS THERE A QUESTION?

A good sense of humor helps everywhere, even in an interview. Everyone is more receptive to an optimistic person than a grouch, but having a sense of humor is not the same as telling jokes. Joke telling in an interview can backfire badly. The interviewer may be humorless, the stress of the moment may cause you to forget the punch line or to tell the joke badly, and no matter what the subject of the joke, it may be offensive to the recruiter or the person he represents.

However, a humorous story, judiciously selected and well told, may work in your favor. It certainly was once a plus for me. I had worked my way through two interviews with my recruiter and four with the company by the time I finally arrived at the decision maker. He was an executive vice president who my recruiter had told me would put me through the toughest interview of my life, and he was living up to his reputation as I flubbed answer after answer and he glared at me.

I had just decided that all was lost when the interviewer said something about knowing your team. Since I was sure everything had gone down the tube anyway, I decided I had nothing to lose. I responded to him with a story I'd heard a few days before. It was about a football coach who had changed teams and was calling all his new players by the wrong names because they were wearing the same numbers as his previous team. It was a great anecdote, really funny, and exactly on point. (But you had to be there.)

It made him laugh out loud, and the change in the atmosphere was almost palpable. It turned out the vice president was a big football fan and was impressed that I knew the coach's name and the teams in question. From that moment on, the interview turned around. If I gave a less-than-ideal answer, he led me along until he got what he wanted.

The company offered me the job, and I learned from an insider that immediately after our interview, the vice president had gone personally to Human Resources to tell them to give me anything I wanted, including a hefty signing bonus. I think in telling that story, I became real to him. My own personality came through, and he liked it.

I turned down the job, though, when a member of the staff told me that four times a year they brought cots into my department so my coworkers and I could work around the clock for three days. I chose self-employment, and even though the vice president called me himself, which was an amazing compliment, I never looked back.

Although you need to be careful with humor, if you have an opportunity to use it and advance your cause at the same time, it might work for you. Then again, it might not. Pick your spot.

Be an interview star:

- Take the interview process seriously and prepare for every aspect
- Keep your focus on how you can contribute to the company, rather than on how the company can serve you
- Demonstrate confidence, courtesy, and professionalism at every meeting
- Be your authentic self
- Listen at least as much as you talk

DO I HAVE TO GO?

SOUNDING SMART IN MEETINGS

Now that you've proven yourself an ace interviewer and landed the job, you meet your coworkers, learn the ropes, and dig into your responsibilities. What's next? Unfortunately, it's probably meetings.

For many people, meetings are the most dreaded part of their jobs. And when management consultants are questioned about the biggest time-wasters their clients face, unnecessary, fruitless meetings are always on the Top Ten list.

Because there are such a variety of alternatives to face-to-face meetings today, many companies are questioning their value, and software is available that calculates the cost of a meeting while it's occurring. The results of those calculations are eye-popping. Depending on the number of participants, the length of the meeting, and the annual salaries of those who attend, it's not unusual for a meeting to cost hundreds of dollars per minute. Some of them are even pricier, and most of them aren't worth it.

Meetings certainly have a place in business. Decisions made

by a group are usually better than those concocted by one person, and when everyone joins in, there's more coordination of activities that follow. Meetings can be a productive exercise in which complex problems are solved, points of view are reconciled, and employees are shown that they are valued. Unfortunately, those meetings seem to exist only in our imagination.

Although you may not be in charge of many meetings, you can help steer them in the right direction. Once you have a good grasp of meeting dynamics, you can be an active, useful participant who helps move the organization's business forward. And that will go a long way toward helping you be recognized and rewarded.

Let's take a bird's-eye view of a typical corporate meeting, in this case the quarterly meeting of the capital expenditure committee at St. Bernville's General Community Hospital and Health Promotion Center. The purpose of this group is to receive requests from various departments for equipment that ranges from a fleet of wheelchairs to a new magnetic resonance imager (MRI).

The president of the hospital is at the head of the table. Also present are Mike Money, the CFO; Elaine Energy, the COO; Nancy Nice, director of nursing; Ron Research, director of marketing; Wendy Word, director of corporate communications; Gilbert Godd, MD, medical director; Larry Learned, DO, director of medical education; Sam Smooth, director of community and media relations; and two senior vice presidents to whom these people report. Eleven people with first-tier salaries. This meeting already costs a bundle and it hasn't even started yet.

The meeting begins with the president's passing out the requests from the various departments; there are fourteen, and they are bound together in the order in which they were received, the oldest request on top. Within the first five minutes, any observer who's still awake can see that the meeting is doomed to failure. Landmines are everywhere; at least a few are going to be detonated, and it's guaranteed that no one's going to sound very smart in this meeting.

Landmine 1: no agenda. Although there is a purpose for the meeting—to make decisions about which capital equipment to approve—no timed agenda has been prepared. Establishing timelines for discussion of agenda items is critical because meetings, just like any other work, expand to fit the time available.

To process fourteen requests could conceivably take seven hours or more, even without any wasted time, and it's already two o' clock. Participants are shuffling their paperwork, reaching for cell phones to cancel the rest of the afternoon, and sinking into despair.

Sam says he has to leave in thirty minutes because of an emergency: A media representative is coming to discuss a rumor that there's been a major drug theft from the hospital pharmacy. As he articulates his exit strategy, Sam silently blesses the reporter who's going to keep him on the hot seat— and out of the meeting—for the next hour.

Wendy has torn her briefing booklet apart and is attempting to place the requests in some order of priority, based on her perceptions of what the public will find most appealing. Ron is staring into space; he's disconnected from the meeting because he's eager to dig into the data analysis that's waiting on his desk.

Landmine 2: lack of preparation. The participants are not ready for this meeting. There's been no planning. Wendy has the right idea as she tries to weight the requests, but she's ranking them according to her own frame of reference. It's the job of the meeting planner to put agenda items in order based on the importance of each item to the whole group, and that can't be done unless the group is consulted prior to the meeting.

The planner should have made sure that attendees had the briefing books far in advance, so they had a chance to study them. The book also might have contained a forced-choice ranking sheet that required each participant to think about the projects and make initial assessments about what should be funded. Comparing the results would have opened the way to fruitful discussion.

The president calls the meeting to order and begins discussion of the first item. It's a request for twenty-five new beds for the oncology service. Mike wonders if any of the old beds can be refurbished and the new beds phased in gradually to level the cash flow over the next couple of years. He is met with dull stares. No one knows.

Landmine 3: the wrong people in the wrong place. Walter Wrench, the facilities manager, whose staff repairs and services hospital property, hasn't been included, so a vital voice is missing. No one from oncology has been asked to participate either, so that valuable perspective also remains unheard.

Wendy, Ron, and Larry probably don't need to be at this meeting; their tasks, if any, can be assigned following the committee's decisions. Right now, however, the entire committee's time is being wasted because little thought has been given to the composition of the group. It's not surprising people are already becoming restless and popping open their laptops to work on other things.

Gilbert Godd mentions that his cousin was a patient in the oncology section recently and that the problems there aren't going to be taken care of by adding new beds. Nancy asks what kinds of problems he's referring to, and the two begin a spirited debate about a staffing shortage and a visiting policy that isn't working. Their wrangle engages the others, and ten minutes go by before the group gets back on task. Eventually, the group agrees to table the request for beds, and they take up the next item.

Landmine 4: hijacking. The meeting leader doesn't know how to regain control of a meeting that's been subverted by a small group. Subtopic discussions may be valid and important for the people involved in them, but they drain attention and energy away from the purpose of the meeting. The group leader must know how to derail topic-killing sidebars and keep the meeting on track.

It's possible that the president, skilled though he may be in other areas, is not a good meeting leader and shouldn't be heading this meeting at all. The task might fall more logically to Elaine, who directly oversees the facility, or Mike, who's more conversant with day-to-day budgetary issues that have an impact on the purchase of equipment. Surely the president should be informed of the committee's decisions, the reasons for them, and the cost-benefit ratios, but attending the meeting itself may not be the best use of his time.

Four hours later, five projects have been approved, nine have been tabled, and the meeting participants have dragged themselves back to their offices, drained, irritated, and in no mood to face the rush-hour traffic.

Everyone was so frustrated at the end of the meeting that no decision was made about what to do next, no postmeeting responsibilities were assigned, and no implementation deadlines were set. All the participants know they'll be dragooned into at least two more horrifying meetings to finish the work that should have been completed in the one they just left—and not one of them relishes the prospect.

Landmine 5: no follow-through. Every meeting must end with an understanding of what was decided, what comes next, and what tasks are assigned to whom. Otherwise, the meeting becomes nothing more than a soap bubble, connected to nothing and floating free until it pops and everyone forgets about it.

SIZE DOESN'T MATTER

The definition of a meeting is broader than simply people gathered in a room to brainstorm, discuss a topic, arrive at a decision, solve a problem, or evaluate options, although these types of meetings still occur every day in every kind of business.

However, in today's time-crunched environment, meetings are just as likely to occur online, by teleconference, in individual offices, or at remote locations. Cell phones are on all day, and wireless communication devices allow us immediate access to e-mail, the Internet, mountains of data, calendars, and much more. Our technology means that we can meet with nearly anyone anytime, either in person or virtually.

Nonetheless, the rules apply to any type of "meeting," from a nationwide sales rally to a drop-by impromptu discussion to a teleconference. A meeting that succeeds is both planned and purposeful.

Let's say you're going down the hall to Victor's office to get his assessment of a potential new hire. Your visit with Victor is a meeting, no matter how short, small, or on the run it appears. Just as you would if you were preparing for a big-room conclave, make sure you:

- Have an agenda, even if it's only one sentence
- Set out a time frame
- Keep the discussion on track
- Summarize and leave when your time is up

You pop into the office. "Victor, do you have ten minutes for me [*setting the time frame*]? I need to speak with you about your opinion of the young man we interviewed yesterday for Serena's position. We're close to a decision on him, and I want your take on a couple of his qualifications [*setting the agenda*]."

Victor is now free to accept or reject your meeting request. He may be working on an agenda of his own—finishing a report or taking a phone call—and not be amenable to another item at this time. However, if he accepts, restrict your conversation to the topic on the table [*keeping the discussion on track*]. What are the qualifications you want to discuss? What are your concerns? On what aspects do you want his opinion? Listen carefully to his answers and at the end of the agreed-upon time, sum up and hightail it out of there. "So you think his extra experience fully makes up for his lack of an advanced degree? I'd really appreciate it if you'd write me a two-line e-mail that summarizes your opinion."

"Let's have lunch next week and talk about other things. I'll e-mail you my times. Thanks for your help [*subsequent tasks, closure*]." That's a darn good meeting.

MEETING BEHAVIOR

The meeting described above is an elementary example. Most meetings involve many different people with divergent points of view, and those meetings may fail for reasons unrelated to the structure of the gathering or the topics discussed. They fail because groups can be held hostage to the antics of those in attendance.

People come to meetings for many reasons: to do the business of the organization, to buff up their own image, to feel a sense of belonging to something bigger than themselves, to push a specific agenda item, to socialize, or even to sabotage the work of others (although most people would deny the last). Intentionally or unintentionally, the saboteurs throw sand in the gears of an otherwise well-oiled meeting. Whether you're the leader or a participant, keeping the meeting moving by using the right words at the right time is a skill essential to your success.

Here are some of the most common sand-throwers. How would you handle them?

Mellifluous Milton dearly loves the sound of his own voice. He talks and talks and talks until everyone's eyes glaze over. He's been at it now for almost five minutes, never yielding the floor and disregarding the body language of others who are trying to enter the conversation. What do you do?

1. Ignore him. Doodle on your paper or play a game on your PDA. Eventually, when he realizes no one is listening, he'll run down.
2. Interrupt and stare at him while you say, "Milton, other people need to talk. You've been on stage for quite a while. Please let someone else say something."
3. Make eye contact and say, "Milton, let me summarize to make sure I'm not missing any points. You're saying that you think the budget portion of the marketing plan for our new products is weak. I helped write that part, so I'm wondering if anyone else has an opinion on it. Trudy, do you agree with Milton?"

4. Make eye contact and say, "Milton, that was a great analysis, but I'd feel much more comfortable with our decision if we analyzed this portion of the plan from several perspectives. Could we hear from other people, too? Susan, what do you think?"

The goal is to stop Milton's domination of the meeting, not to attack him personally. The more ignored or challenged he feels, the more—and more forcefully—he'll hog the floor. In most cases, the best response is 3, and any member of the group can make this kind of statement. If there's no change in behavior, the leader may have to step in with some variation of response 4, indicating that as much as the group values Milton's point of view, the importance of the discussion requires that everyone participate.

Confrontational Carl has to be right. He'll fight on forever, challenging every member of the group until he gains universal acceptance for his positions. He's a put-down artist, always negative, always implying that those who don't agree with him aren't very smart or have no principles. Unlike Milton, who's just a pain, Carl can be dangerous in a meeting. While people are defending themselves against his attacks, they can't attend to the business at hand, and the whole meeting fizzles. During the last hour, Carl has interrupted others several times with his own brand of sarcasm, and the group is becoming demoralized. How do you react?

1. Point your finger at him and say, "Carl, you're wrong and everyone here is tired of being berated by you. Shut up."
2. Make eye contact and say, "Carl, we're all on the same team here, but that doesn't mean we're going to agree on every point. I certainly respect your opinion, but by listening to everyone, we make better decisions."
3. Make eye contact and say, "Carl, I'm interested in having you expand your thoughts about the goals portion of the marketing plan. Can you give us a specific statement of what you consider especially objectionable?"

4. Look at the leader and say, "Could we take a short break and get back together in a few minutes?"

Carl is a classic intimidator, and underneath it all, intimidators are often insecure people who've never felt heard. Although response 1 is certainly a temptation, confronting intimidators head-on and challenging their "rightness" makes for even greater opposition. Pointing a finger in someone's face is aggressive and only intensifies the belligerence.

Response 2 helps connect Carl to the group, and response 3 defuses the situation by distracting him from wide-ranging attacks, focusing him on one issue, and giving him the floor for a discrete period of time. If Carl veers from the topic in a free-form harangue, you can bring him back to reality by saying, "I hear that, Carl, but I'm primarily interested in your take on the goals." If things are really getting out of hand, you might have to resort to response 4 so the leader can bring the situation back under control.

During the break, the leader should seek out Carl for a private chat and state the expectations she has for the meeting: everyone is listened to with respect, and personal attacks are not part of the agenda for the day. If you are the leader, you might say, "Carl, I see the group refusing to participate because they don't want to be put down and made to feel that their contributions are unimportant. I'd appreciate it if you would allow others to speak without interruption, and I'd like you to treat them with the same courtesy I expect from them in speaking to you."

In this example, the leader spoke carefully. She did not attack Carl directly with words such as, "**You** are creating havoc in there and everyone is furious. Can't **you** see how obnoxious **you** are?" Instead, she sent a clear message that consisted of what she had observed ("**I** see . . .") and what she wanted to see ("**I'd** appreciate . . ."). This gentle approach may not always work, but it's far more likely to elicit a positive response than trying to fight fire with fire.

Digressing Danny cannot seem to stay on topic, no matter what. He's been sidetracking the discussion of the marketing plan with anecdotes that are only tangentially related to the issue. Because Danny happens to be a great storyteller, everyone is listening and laughing and having a great time, but the meeting has ground to a standstill and time slippage has become an issue. How do you handle it?

1. Make eye contact and say, "Oh, gosh, Danny, what a great story! But we're falling far behind our agenda. I have a conference call in less than an hour, and I'd like to make sure we get through our discussion so we don't have to call another meeting."
2. Roll your eyes and say to the person next to you, "There he goes again!"
3. Point at your agenda, glare, and say, "Could we please get back to this item? I don't have all day."
4. Take a bathroom break and hope he's stopped talking by the time you come back.

In fact, responses 1 and 3 say the same thing, except that one is polite and respectful and the other is unnecessarily harsh.

Multitasking Maggie is present only in body. She gives scant attention to what's going on because she's answering e-mail, listening to voice mail messages, and proofreading the latest draft of a report that's due tomorrow. What to do?

1. Make eye contact and say, "Earth to Maggie. Did you hear what Elroy had to say? What's your response? He was talking about your department."
2. Make eye contact and say, "Good Lord, Maggie. Can't you disconnect for a few minutes and pay some attention to the rest of us? We have other work to do, too. Let's get this meeting out of the way."
3. Make eye contact and say, "Maggie, what do you think of Elroy's observations about the wording of section 3? It seems to me your perspective might be different from his, and I'd love to hear your take on it."
4. Ignore her as much as she's ignoring everyone else.

Response 4 is obviously counterproductive, since the idea is to reengage Maggie and gain her cooperation. Response 1 is supercilious and mean spirited. Response 2 is also unkind, but response 3 might work nicely.

Multitasking is a huge issue. A study commissioned by Raindance Communications found that 90 percent of audio-conference participants did things besides pay attention to the call. Seventy percent worked on other projects, 51 percent read e-mail, 38 percent ate, 36 percent took other calls, and 13 percent participated in the call from the bathroom.[1] What a waste of time and brainpower!

Although time management experts talk glowingly about doing two things at once, they mean combining two low-effort tasks: reading the newspaper while toasting a bagel. However, trying to meld two engrossing tasks, such as sending e-mail while fully participating in an important discussion, is a recipe for inefficiency. In addition, it's discourteous to the meeting leader and other attendees who are not getting the best efforts from those who are multitasking. Unfortunately, those who multitask on the phone have now brought this impolite behavior to in-person meetings.

If you're leading the meeting, it might be wise to take Maggie aside during a break. You could then say, "Maggie, I see you working so hard at so many things. I can excuse you from the meeting if you need to be somewhere else, but I think you have valuable insights to offer. It would help me and the group if, for the duration of the meeting, you could give us your full attention. The marketing plan is important to the whole organization."

In fact, meeting ground rules in any organization should forbid the use of cell phones, laptops, PDAs, or any other distracting technology except in the service of the meeting itself. No games, no picture taking, no Internet searching during the meeting. Emergencies must be attended to, of course, but not that many arise during the course of a two-hour meeting.

Jumpy Jennifer hates what she calls analysis paralysis. She's very smart, well prepared for every meeting, and wants to get on with decision making. She drums her fingers, seems impatient with others' contributions, and checks her watch every few minutes. "Can we vote yet?" is her mantra. Discussion on one section of the marketing plan has lasted less than ten minutes and she's already calling for a decision. How do you respond?

1. Make eye contact and say, "Jennifer, please. We all know you're ready to vote, but the rest of us aren't."
2. Stare at her and say, "I'm not going to be stampeded just because you have a lunch appointment or something. Relax, for Pete's sake."
3. Make eye contact and say, "Jennifer, the last time you insisted on a quick vote, the results were disastrous, if you remember."
4. Make eye contact and say, "Hey, Jennifer, I've noticed you can gather facts quickly and like to move to closure, but some of us aren't quite that fast. I'd like to examine more options so I'm comfortable with our decision. Our agenda says we have more time. What does everyone else think?"

Response 4 or something like it is the most useful one. A statement that recognizes differences among meeting participants, without making value judgments on which style is "best," validates everyone, even Jennifer. The other choices are insulting and unkind.

COMMUNICATION STYLES

Meetings may bog down even if every participant is prepared and eager to arrive at good decisions; they can collapse because people are people, not cattle. They deal with information in various ways. Some concentrate on here-and-now decisions; others are more concerned with long-term ramifications. Some are planners, some are doers. Some people gain energy from being in a group and from testing ideas for hours;

others can do group work for a while but then must get away and think quietly.

Some people need facts and data to make decisions; others react more to anecdotes and case examples. Early in my career, I occasionally was called upon to present marketing ideas to a group composed primarily of male physicians. I would make my presentation, they would shoot everything down, and I would go away muttering.

One day, I happened to be in the department chairman's office; he said he thought one of my ideas might have merit, but "don't give me all that garbage about perceived need. If you think something should be done, show me the numbers. Tell me where it's worked somewhere else and back up your recommendations with some evidence I can see. I'm not a touchy-feely person."

I discovered that his was the majority position. The next time I went to seek support from the group for a project, I brought facts: national statistics, local statistics, and trend data. The guys jumped all over them. I fielded more questions and heard more discussion than ever before, and I walked out with approval for the project. Just as I got to the door, the chairman gave me a big thumbs-up. My performance had demonstrated that not only had I heard what he said, but I'd also done something about it. He was an ally of mine from that day on.

A former officemate of mine at a woman's health center says,

Our staff was all women, and we were all big-picture people, very much into the *what* and not too concerned with *how* things got done. One day we were planning the grand opening of the center. We had flip charts and people taking notes and all the other things you're supposed to have for effective meetings.

Ideas were flowing and we were excited. In the middle of all this discussion, our administrative assistant suddenly said, "How many chairs should we order and how much parking should I try to reserve?"

The conversation came to a dead stop. Not one of

us had given the first thought to how many people this event might draw and that at some point at least a few of them might want to sit down. Our assistant had been very quiet because that was her nature and also because once our group got rolling, we could be over-whelming. But Sally had an insight none of us had considered. Once she had our attention, she asked a barrage of other practical questions. It was an object lesson for us, and after that we always sought her opin-ions. She was the one detail-oriented, feet-on-the-ground person in the whole place.

Style differences can erect barriers between people; understanding how the other person thinks does much to eliminate such roadblocks. Committees and workgroups usu-ally contain a mixture of styles, and so-called creatives—advertising, marketing, and public relations people—often view an agenda item from a different perspective than com-mittee members from finance and operations.

When I worked in hospital administration, I used to butt heads with one particular member of the staff. He was a good guy, but in a lot of ways, we just didn't understand each other. I wondered why we so often seemed to be on opposite sides.

One day we had a staff retreat and we all took a test that was supposed to tell us which hemisphere of the brain we used most often and whether we were predominantly rational and analytic or holistic and intuitive. The consultant who gave the test had us sit in chairs from right to left around the room, based on our scores. I was so far to the right, I actually was out the door in the hall, and when I looked at the farthest left chair, there was Bob. We waved at each other.

Everyone watching us simply broke up, because it was so clear why he and I couldn't find common ground. He was a detail-oriented, linear, analytic scholar, and I was an off-the-wall, divergent thinker. He reasoned things through to the end. I liked to churn out ideas as fast as possible and have some-body else worry about the details.

Bob and I laughed pretty hard, too. We saw that our issues weren't personal, and after this test, we understood each other better. I was able to listen to his concerns much more easily, and he was more receptive to what I had to say.

One of the most potentially frustrating style differences arises between what are often referred to as "matchers" and "mismatchers": matchers see and perceive similarities; mismatchers see and perceive differences.

Show a matcher two pink balls with purple polka dots and he or she will tell you all the ways the objects are similar: they're spherical, the same color, and decorated the same way. Give a mismatcher a look at the same objects and you'll learn that the shades of pink are slightly different, three of the polka dots are bigger than the rest, and one of the objects is significantly heavier than the other.

Matchers tend to be agreeable, go-along-to-get-along folks, more conventional in their thinking. Mismatchers are more likely to keep things stirred up with questions and challenges to the group wisdom because they see discrepancies and potentially thorny issues. Because of mismatchers' sometimes confrontational style, groups can view them as obstreperous, divisive, and just plain annoying.

If you mix these two types in a meeting, conflict is almost inevitable, but it's wise to give some heed to the mismatcher. Groups composed only of matchers can make bad choices just to get the work done. They're so busy avoiding conflict and reaching the easy agreement that they may not raise or discuss critical or dissenting opinions.

It's important to differentiate a mismatcher, whose sometimes abrasive style can result in more carefully considered group decisions, from a Confrontational Carl, whose only interest is in finding fault with everyone else's opinions and grabbing control of the meeting. You can sometimes rein in his behavior by gaining consensus from other members of the group one by one, until the negative member is isolated and outnumbered. You can state your position and then say, "What do you think, Don?" "Do you agree, Melissa?" (As long as you ask in a casual and congenial way, the leader is not likely to view you as usurping his role. If fact, he may admire your initiative in helping to keep the meeting productive.)

RECOGNIZING ANOTHER STYLE DIFFERENCE

Skilled speakers and listeners will tell you that we all give clues about what kind of thinking style we prefer. Those clues are found in telltale words.

Let's say you're trying to make a point in a meeting. Another attendee says, "I just don't see what you're getting at." In this case, *see* is the telltale word. This person probably has what Linda Kreger Silverman, PhD, calls a visual-spatial orientation;[2] he thinks primarily in pictures rather than words. To reach this type of people, don't unleash a torrent of verbiage. Try a diagram or some other kind of visual aid. You could also say, "Let's try to picture it this way. It's like . . . ," and then use a visual-verbal example to make your point.

Suppose another member of the group says, "I don't hear anything about this project that appeals to me. I don't understand everyone's enthusiasm." What are the telltale words? *Hear* and *understand*. This person, like most of the population, has a preference for the auditory-sequential style and probably needs more conversation to grasp your point.

Drawing a picture or showing a slide, as you might do for the visual person, won't be effective with these listeners and might even make them impatient. A better response would be to say, "Perhaps a little more discussion will be useful. Have the rest of you heard anything that makes you think this project might be of value?" Presenting your ideas step by step is also a helpful strategy because sequential types learn by piling fact on fact.

And after all this, another participant chimes in, saying, "It just doesn't feel right. I can't wrap my head around this whole idea." This person's telltale words—*feel* and *wrap*—tip off a kinesthetic learner, that is, a person who likes to touch and manipulate things and deals better with ideas if you can present them concretely. You might demonstrate a point by using a model that the person can hold and examine.

I once sat in on a sales pitch with a man who was trying to sell modular construction to solve an overcrowding problem. He brought along simply illustrated wooden blocks to demonstrate how the modules could be stacked and combined on the several different building sites. It was fascinating to watch the reactions of the participants. Some of them never touched the blocks, but the kinesthetic types gravitated to them, moving them in different configurations and trying various combinations of sizes and heights. This group also warmed to the modular concept much faster than the others at the meeting.

When you're dealing with questions or objections, accommodating the communication styles of the other participants often makes them feel understood and more willing to continue exploring an idea. When you know your group includes a mixed bag of styles, you can prepare an oral presentation with a whiteboard illustration or a slide or two for those who learn through their ears and eyes; give some thought to how you'll demonstrate your idea to the kinesthetic attendees.

AN OVERLOOKED STRATEGY

In any meeting, it's important not only to have a variety of viewpoints and styles represented, but also an assortment of group dynamics skills. Meetings don't have to include only those with a vested interest in the topics under discussion, although you don't want to include so many people that the meeting becomes unwieldy and expensive. Throwing different people into the mix can add substance to a meeting.

If you know that Rita is a superb consensus builder, try to have her invited to a meeting that might be contentious, even if she has no stake in the items being discussed. Tell her why she's being asked so she'll be on the alert for opportunities to exercise her peace-making abilities.

Some people are adept at observing the process, rather than the content, of a meeting; they can easily spot potential role conflicts, budding coalitions, and hidden motivations. Process observers don't participate in the business of the meeting, but they watch how the group functions. They often can see more clearly than the participants whether the meeting is wandering off track and if everyone is contributing. They can perceive behaviors that either close down discussion or improve the flow of communication.

Usually, process observers are given some time to present their thoughts about the dynamics of the group; the purpose of their comments is to provide midcourse correction and make future group interactions more productive. Process observation requires some training, but most people can learn to do it. Group members can rotate in the process observation role or an outsider can be asked to provide the service. If your meetings aren't as productive as you'd like, inviting someone to observe the process can be useful.

Moreover, if you suggest such an arrangement and it improves the quality of meetings, your superiors will probably appreciate your contribution and be impressed that you thought of it.

THE NUMBER ONE MEETING SKILL

Often the most important thing you can do in a meeting is zip your lip. Not, of course, when you're asked for a contribution or you have something important to get on the record. However, it is sometimes valuable to sit still and listen intently. By tuning in to what people say, tuning out distractions, and watching body language, you may notice things others don't. If you're attentive and quiet as the meeting progresses, you may hear areas of commonality in seemingly disparate opinions. You may discern a style conflict and be able to help people understand one another better. Or summarize a discussion that's become too complicated. All these skills are important arrows to have in your quiver, but they remain undeveloped if you don't first learn to listen.

Rate Your Listening Ability

When you're attending a meeting, do you

	Yes	No
1. Find yourself thinking of your response before you've heard everything the other people have to say?	☐	☐
2. Interrupt frequently and finish the others' sentences for them?	☐	☐
3. Decide quickly which members of the group are "right" or "wrong "and tell them why?	☐	☐
4. Become angry or upset if someone disagrees with you?	☐	☐
5. Doodle, look out the window, turn your chair away from the other speakers, examine your manicure, or check your messages when others are speaking?	☐	☐
6. Forget to verify what you think you heard the other person say?	☐	☐

A "yes" to two or more questions means it's time to polish your listening skills. Sounding intelligent always begins with listening.

The first key to good listening is to pay full attention to the speaker, and this is a difficult thing to do. Experts tell us that we hear about half of what other people say because our minds are so busy rehearsing what we're going to say in response. We interrupt others and finish their sentences for them so we can get to the important part of the conversation, which, of course, is what *we* have to say. And if we're hearing only half of what's being communicated, we're setting ourselves up for confusing interactions, time-consuming false starts, and needless confrontations.

Slow down and concentrate on listening. Recognize that others may think or speak at a more measured pace than you do. Before you request clarification, question facts, or criticize, even constructively, take the time to make sure the speaker has made all of her important points and finished speaking. To listen effectively, we have to give others the time they need to express themselves and to silence our own words, both those we speak and the ones we're playing in our heads. However, it's acceptable to jot down notes while another is speaking so you can respond appropriately when it's your turn.

Second, weigh ideas instead of judging people. Most of us spend a great deal of time making judgments about others. He's an idiot. She's too political. He's brilliant. She's only out for herself. When those judgments color our listening—when we decide an idea is good or bad because we like or don't like the person who expresses it—our emotions have taken over rational thought. Debate is no longer about issues. It's about personalities, and basing business decisions on whether someone else's personality appeals to you is not good policy. Even a blind pig can turn over a truffle, and even someone whose personality you find repugnant may have a business-saving idea.

It's important, especially if your emotions are engaged, to make sure you hear what the speaker actually said and not what you thought she said. For example, suppose you operate a successful store and want to add a second location. You and a great many other people have spent weeks looking for a location. You believe you've found the right one.

Frank, a member of your advisory board, is raising both objections and your blood pressure. He seems to be suggesting it would be a good idea for you and your task group to go back to the beginning and find another site. The very thought of that makes you so anxious you're not sure you're hearing him properly. It's time for a clarity check.

You might say, "Frank, am I correct that you're saying we

should consider another location for the new store?" Frank may say that's exactly what he means, and then you're in a position to ask him to spell out his reservations in more detail. His reasons may be valid, and you may indeed have to think about other options.

However, he may surprise you by responding, "No, that's not what I said. I think the location is fine, but your team needs to look more carefully at the demographics to see if you should refine your product mix for that particular store. Abington Heights has been your anchor store, but you're going to have to change your offerings for Charing Woods. Even though they're similar communities, they have very different types of consumers. I think if you go generic or just replicate what you have in Abington Heights, the Charing Woods store will fail." Your asking for clarity has saved the meeting from veering off in an unproductive direction and kept you from exploding at an inopportune time. And, by the way, exploding at any time does nothing to advance an argument or enhance others' perception of you.

Third, adjust your gaze and your posture. To enhance listening, look directly at those who are speaking. Don't stare, however. A fixed, unblinking gaze is unnerving, but eye contact is important. Research conducted at Queen's University in Kingston, Ontario, Canada, found a "strong link between the amount of eye contact people receive and their degree of participation in group communications."[3] It didn't matter whether the eye contact was received when the speaker was speaking or at other times during the conversation. To increase group interaction, keep your eyes on the prize—and on the other attendees.

Last, a relaxed, open posture conveys that you're engaged and ready to listen, especially if you lean in slightly toward the speaker. However, don't move in so close that you invade other people's personal space. As they try to establish a more comfortable distance, they're unable to participate in any kind of meaningful conversation. An occasional nod to show your concurrence with a speaker's point indicates that you haven't checked out of the discussion, but it's not necessary to look like a bobblehead doll—even if you vigorously agree.

NOW SPEAK UP

Because you've listened, observed, and taken the time to learn something about the other participants' communication styles, you're ready to make your own significant contributions to any meeting and to establish yourself as someone of value and importance. Below is a list of some of the most critical touchpoints of any meeting and what you might say at these important junctures.

Touchpoint 1: establishing purpose. This is an A-1 task. If expectations for the meeting are unclear, attendees can wander far afield and take little substantive action on important issues. What you might say:

> The agenda didn't clearly outline what needs to happen today. Are we to decide how to staff a new department or figure out ways to reassign tasks so a new department isn't necessary? I'd like to make sure we're all talking about the same thing.

Touchpoint 2: summarizing. Summarizing in a concise manner serves several purposes: it keeps participants from plowing the same ground again and again, focuses attention on the issues still to be resolved, and can stop discussion if there's nothing further to be gained from it. Here are three examples of good summaries:

> Here's where I think we are. Marketing wants to do a survey of customer attitudes, but Martha's department wants to get the new product on the shelves within sixty days. They believe our customer experience over the past five years gives us all the data we need and that the price point is right. John's suggesting a com-

promise: a test run of the product at four locations. Is that right?

I'd like to table this item. The discussion seems to be going around in a circle, and I think the reason for that is that we're missing some pivotal pieces of information. Some of us think an outside consultant might be able to fill in the blanks, but we haven't identified who that person might be. It seems to me we're unprepared to move ahead today. Let's identify our consultant, get his input, and then come back when we have everything we need to make a good decision.

We've spent a great deal of time on this today, but we can't seem to get to consensus. Let's think about how we might do that and revisit this whole topic at our next meeting.

Touchpoint 3: looking for agreement. Occasionally a meeting loses momentum because two people or groups are locked in a death grip. However, there's almost always some point on which they can agree. If you can identify and summarize agreements, even if they're small ones, you might be able to move the meeting away from the point of contention. What you might say:

It seems to me we're at a bit of an impasse. We're talking about adding a twenty-four-hour helpline to our services. The disagreement seems to center on how to staff it. Rosa, you want to keep the jobs in house. Hector, you think it's more economical to turn them over to a subcontractor.

What interests me is that you've both spoken in favor of the helpline itself. What we need to know is whether we can get past the disagreement you've identified. Hector, can you see any point of Rosa's argument as valid? Rosa, is there any part of Hector's position that seems reasonable? Do you think it would help if we put together a small task group to work only on finding a solution to this problem? Maybe we could come up with something that's agreeable to both of you.

Touchpoint 4: reaching consensus. Sometimes a group has made a decision, but they don't know it yet. If you sense general acceptance of an idea, you can help move the meeting forward. What you might say:

I'm hearing that we're in agreement because we're already talking about how to carry out our decision. To make everything official, could we have a vote and move on to the next agenda item?

Touchpoint 5: ending the meeting. Ending a meeting is another high-priority moment. Participants must be aware of what's been decided and if there are actions that must be taken subsequent to the meeting. A person who ties up the loose endings of the meeting is of great value to those whose minds might have wandered. What you might say:

I'd like to make sure I'm completely clear on what we've done here. It seems we've reached consensus on the store issue and tabled the discussion of the new department. Hector and Rosa have agreed to put together a group to make recommendations about the personnel concerns for the helpline. Is that right? Have I missed anything?

SPEAKING WITH AUTHORITY

No matter how brilliant your contributions might be, how you present yourself can enhance or detract from what you're trying to accomplish in the meeting. You want to sound self-assured but not overbearing; welcoming to all points of view but not indecisive. To maintain that balance:

Don't waffle. If an idea is worth presenting, it's worth presenting strongly. "I think we should . . ." or "I suggest . . ." has a much different ring from a tentative, "This may not be the best solution, but maybe we should consider . . ."

Look at your audience. Speak to those around the conference table, not to the table itself. If you get nervous in meetings, spend some time in front of a mirror or with a close friend practicing and perfecting a more self-confident demeanor. Business meetings are for adults, so it's time to get your head up and your toe out of the sand.

Don't substitute a question for a statement. "Do you think we should . . . ?" positions you as a supplicant. "We should . . ." positions you as a leader. And don't present your solution and then say, "OK?" You don't have to ask for criticism; the group will provide it. The only time you might hedge is if you want to stimulate a discussion. In that case, you can provide a suggestion that's not your best shot and invite others to build on the idea. But don't make a habit of it. In most cases, you want to lead from strength.

Don't uptalk. Uptalking is using a rising inflection to end sentences that aren't questions. Listen in on any conversation among teen girls and you'll hear almost nonstop uptalk. For this age group, uptalk is a sign of belonging. It's acceptable in that context, no matter how annoying it may be to parents or teachers who have to listen to it all day. Adults, especially adult women, should break the uptalk habit because it's much too tentative. It appears that you're asking permission to share your opinions rather than stating them with conviction ("So I think we should relocate our server to building 3?").

Watch your body language. If you're standing, stand firmly on both feet, but not at military attention. If you're sitting, sit straight but not stiffly. Be careful in the ways you use your hands. An inclusive, open-handed gesture is welcoming; other gestures, such as stabbing a finger in the direction of your listeners or holding your palm up in the "stop" position can be interpreted as aggressive.

Handle interruptions and don't tolerate abuse. You can

deal with interruptions tactfully: "Let me get to the end of what I have to say. That might answer your question." Abuse or bullying is another issue. Unfortunately, there are some people who delight in tearing others down in front of a group—yelling at them, disparaging their ideas, and questioning their competence. They're Confrontational Carl squared.

When confronted with a bully, silence is, at first, a potent ally. Don't be drawn in. Sit or stand quietly, with a neutral expression on your face. Let the ranter rant until he runs down; do not respond. When he's quiet, calmly continue with your points. The group will probably discipline the disruptive member if he starts up again.

If heckling continues, be more assertive, but don't answer aggression with aggression, no matter how attractive that prospect may seem. Keep your messages positive. Say what you see. Say what you want. "Jesse, I see you're not interested in my idea. I've noted your comments for later discussion, but now I'd like to continue without interruption."

Sometimes, no matter how assertive you are, a bully like this will keep coming back at you with objections or caustic criticisms. Here are some things to remember:

Don't allow the bully to undermine your sense of self. As Eleanor Roosevelt once said, "No one can make you feel inferior without your permission," so hold your head up, look him in the eye, and refuse to be cowed.

Consider the context. Does Jesse act this way with everyone in every situation or is his behavior in this meeting unusual? If he's generally a nice guy, and he's out of character right now, perhaps he has a problem that's gnawing at him and simply venting at whoever crosses his path. If he's always rude to you, but nice to others, then you two have a problem that needs to be addressed in another forum. If he's wretched to everyone all the time, that's a management concern, not a personal issue.

Draw the line firmly. If the bully crosses over from attacking your ideas to attacking you, protect yourself. You may feel that you shouldn't have to fight back in a public meeting, so if you prefer, you can ask the leader to restore order. Should the leader also be intimidated, you'll have to take the upper hand. "Jesse, you have a lot of expertise I respect, and I want to incorporate that in our discussion of the issue. I'm asking you to confine your comments to what we're talking about, rather than making me the subject."

If he continues, you may have no choice but to shut down the discussion. "Jesse, I think you and I have reached the end of useful conversation, and I don't permit anyone to speak to me so disrespectfully. I'm going to move on now. Rich, do you have anything you'd like to say?"

When meetings are necessary, they don't have to be torturous events. By attending to the people and the process, respecting all opinions, and speaking confidently when it's

---

The No-Meeting Option

Many times we hold meetings for reasons that are less than compelling. Try to call off or avoid a meeting if:

- There are only one or two decisions to be made and little discussion is required. Save time and money; suggest that decisions be made by conference call or e-mail ballot.
- The only business of the meeting is updates. Ask for information to read before the next meeting.
- The meeting is scheduled, but no one has submitted an agenda item. Guess what? Nobody cares. If you feel the meeting is necessary, you'll have to argue for it more persuasively, because a lack of agenda items is a glaring signal that others don't share your enthusiasm.
- The meeting is a habit that should be broken. In many cases, a weekly staff meeting is a waste of time, especially if the staff is small and works together closely every day. Every other week, once a month, or even quarterly may be enough.

your turn, you can help make meetings effective and maybe even enjoyable. Eventually management will notice your contribution and might even thank you for it.

Be a meeting star:

- Focus on the purpose of the meeting
- Be an active participant
- Present ideas in more than one way
- Help to keep the meeting on track
- Listen at least as much as you talk

9

IN THE OFFICE

SOUNDING SMART EVERY DAY

Advancement in a career often depends on both your expertise and your ability to present yourself in a positive manner—that is, what you accomplish *and* how you come across in the day-to-day environment of your job. Being able to speak fluently and intelligently builds your confidence in facing the kinds of situations you encounter regularly: pitching an idea to a boss or committee; asking for a raise, more responsibility, or a transfer; and confronting naysayers, bullies, difficult colleagues, and even your boss. Knowing the right thing to say also helps you deal effectively with sensitive issues on the job.

IT'S A GREAT IDEA

A client's problem is not something to be feared. It's an opportunity for you to shine.

Here's a typical scenario: You're a relatively new associate in an advertising firm with two principals and a staff of account executives. You have been assigned to rebrand a well-known consumer product for a younger audience. Because you're young yourself, you have an edge. You understand how this particular market thinks and speaks. You've worked with the marketing arm of your agency to get a sense of what the intended audience already thinks of the product—and the news isn't wonderful. The target market knows the product well but considers it old and stodgy.

You've come up with a slogan and campaign that's very hip, very cool, and works brilliantly against the current stuffy image. You've worked with the art department to design new packaging that gives the product an updated look. The agency principals like the concept and invite you to pitch it to the client. Both principals will be at the meeting, but you're expected to make the presentation.

This presentation has the potential to launch your career—to take you from your desk in the cubicle farm to an account executive's office—but if you perform poorly, you might end up writing headlines for a long time. You must remember to:

- *Acknowledge* the opportunity the principals have given you and thank them for it.
- *Look and sound like a professional,* not a recent graduate who hasn't yet mastered the language of business. Even though you're pitching an idea for a young market, the people you're pitching to are older executives. Dress appropriately; discard trendy expressions and flip attitudes.
- *Put the client's needs first.* The presentation is not your personal platform; it's a way to bring the client new ideas and new business.
- *Project a competent, confident attitude,* but steer clear of self-aggrandizement. You want to come across as an expert, not an arrogant know-it-all.
- *Prepare for several outcomes:* the client loves the idea; the client hates the idea; the client is less than wowed, but not completely turned off.

Whether you're about to pitch a product or an intangible, all such presentations have some elements in common:

A brief statement of the problem, with supporting details.

A presentation of the solution, with the benefits highlighted and objections met. All new ideas involve some degree of risk or change, and most people resist both. What strong points can you make that will override this innate resistance?

Opportunities for comment. As in every other aspect of business, listening is critical. Who jumps on the idea? Who runs away from it? What are their reasons and motives? Does anyone raise critical points you haven't considered? Can you answer the concerns adequately?

Refinement of the idea. Build on the comments of the others. Can you incorporate their ideas into your final model and thus gain more widespread support? People who feel they've been heard are more likely to take up the challenge of a new idea.

Acceptance or rejection of the idea. If your idea is accepted, have you thought through the steps necessary to implement it? Are you ready to move quickly? If the idea goes down in flames, can you put your finger on why? Did you misjudge your audience or was it a timing problem? Is the idea dead or just in need of resuscitation at a later date?

When pitching an idea like this, it's impossible to be overprepared. You must have facts, data, and information at your fingertips. One of the most important uses of this information is to anticipate and counter your clients' objections without being condescending and impatient.

The morning of your presentation, the client arrives. As you enter the room, you wait to be introduced by your bosses before launching into your idea. You shake hands, make eye contact, smile, and tell the client how pleased and happy you are that the principals of the agency have entrusted you with this presentation. And then you begin.

As you know, Mr. Green and Ms. White assigned me to come up with some concepts that will rebrand your product for a younger market. You've told us that you're concerned about the long-term sales of your product. We agree that you're right to have those concerns. Baby boomers are your biggest customers, but the oldest boomers are now turning sixty, so to maintain sales stability over the next couple of decades, we all need to think about appealing to younger market segments. [*statement of the problem*]

What we know about your potential customers is both good and bad. They consider your product to be effective, safe, and well priced. However, they identify it with their parents, and in some cases even with their grandparents, and that turns them off.

Because the product is well regarded, I think you have a great opportunity to capture a younger customer base. You don't have to rethink your entire product because it already has a fine reputation; you simply need to develop a parallel campaign to the one you run for baby boomers and run the campaign in media that target this population. You'll also need to beef up your presence on the World Wide Web. You're not active on the Web, and to reach these consumers you'll have to be very visible there. We have specialists here who can design inventive ways to make that happen. [*supporting details and description of the environment*]

The benefits of this campaign are enormous. Simply by developing specific, targeted messages, you have the opportunity to capture an entirely new market. Once they try the product, its safety and quality will bind them, just the way it has bound their parents. It's a cost-effective campaign that will work now and far into the future. Here are the slogan, sample copy, and some options for redesigning the packaging. [*selling the benefits*]

Your clients sit quietly for a moment, and then they begin to pick the idea apart. Don't become defensive or take their objections personally. This is the point of the presentation where resistance comes into play, and it's where your preparation in countering objections will stand you in good stead.

Don't act as if the objections are silly or beneath you. Take each one seriously and answer it carefully. For example, perhaps the client says that running two advertising tracks is too expensive.

"That's a concern, I know, but this campaign will have legs. You won't have to reinvent it every two months, so you'll save money in the long run. We also believe that you'll recover all your costs within a year or so. We know this campaign will have great long-term effectiveness; we've done some generic focus group research with younger consumers, and the concept tested very well across the board. A clear majority of participants indicated they would try a product with attributes similar to yours."

The client then says, "The market-segmenting idea sounds really intriguing to me, but it seems too ambitious."

"It *is* ambitious, and I wouldn't want to roll out a completely segmented campaign right away. It's something to build toward after we consult with our multicultural advisors. Different ethnic groups may require different key messages. I think it's important to reach out, though, and bring these segments into the campaign. The United States is more diverse than ever before, and there are huge, rapidly growing markets we've never courted before. Within a very few years, the African American population will be close to one trillion dollars in yearly consumer spending, and they aren't big users of your product. If we can convert a portion of those consumers, you'll see rapid growth in sales. And that success can be replicated in other segments."

After answering questions, you move in with your best point. "I've talked this over with Mr. Green and Mr. White, and they've suggested to me that this idea is simply the opening wedge in a long-term strategy." [*listening, meeting objections, and refining*]

By involving the principals, you add a layer of credibility and also indicate that the agency has thought through an entire strategy rather than one short-term tactic. You show your superiors appropriate deference, and they buttress you with the authority of their position. They are now in a position to lay out the broader strategy you mentioned.

If the client rejects the idea out of hand, don't look hangdog. Don't slam your portfolio on the table in a fit of pique. Far better to respond this way: "Would you be interested in trying out the idea in a limited way? I think it would be good to test it in three bellwether markets. That way we can work out any bugs at a much less expensive stage of development, and if we get the results we expect, we're ready to go on the national campaign. I have a great deal of faith that we'll hit or exceed our target numbers."

At this point, you also invite the agency principals to join the discussion because you can't simply grab the test market project; it must be given to you. Your bosses probably will be impressed that you didn't let the meeting get away from you and participate willingly in further conversation. At that point, you've become a team in the client's eyes and in your bosses' estimation as well. You're an official rising star.

When you've hit a home run, enjoy the moment but resist the idea of congratulating yourself. Focus immediately on how the idea can be implemented and set a time frame, once again involving the principals, who will be the ones to assign teams and tasks. Don't overreach your authority.

It's likely the client will ask to think about what you've presented. This is not the time to be impatient; very few ideas are accepted immediately, so be realistic about your chances for quick success. Be gracious and offer to set up further meetings and discussion. [acceptance, rejection, or waiting]

When the meeting is over, it's wise to ask for feedback from your superiors. How do they think things went? What did you do well? What do you need to work on to improve your presentations? Seeking advice from more experienced colleagues is never weak, and what they tell you may be invaluable. Learning from mentors also shows humility, which makes it less likely that higher-ups will consider you a threat if they promote you to a position of greater responsibility.

Sometimes a pitch is three people sitting at a conference table; at other times there may be twenty people in the room. Your visual aids may be as simple as a sketch on scratch paper; to present more complicated ideas, you might need slides, handouts, or models. No matter how simple or complex the pitch, however, the basic process is the same, and once you've tried it a few times, you'll become continually better at it, making you a standout. Showing initiative and working toward effective, innovative solutions is in everyone's best interest and will please those who have the power to promote you.

Quick Tip: Show Some Excitement

Enthusiasm sells. Most people dislike an overwrought pitch, so don't shout and wave your arms around like a pinwheel. On the other hand, don't be so low-key and businesslike that you put your listeners to sleep. What you say is important, but so is how you say it. Use vocal variety to animate your ideas and engage your listeners.

RAISES AND RESPONSIBILITIES

You've been working hard for at least a year at your agreed-upon initial salary. Your superiors have complimented you on your professional manner, efficiency, and good ideas. You decide it's time to ask for a raise. Doing so can be a nail-biting experience, but you can pull it off effectively if you remember some basic tenets:

Pick the right time. How's the business doing? You can get financial information about a public company from inside the company itself or go online to find the data. In a privately held company, you'll have to read the signals a little more carefully; for example, if your company has just announced a massive layoff or fired a bunch of top-level managers, that's a pretty strong indicator that cash is tight. However, if business is expanding, you're in a better position to negotiate for your share of the increase.

Once you've ascertained the general health of the company, choose the most opportune time to go after your raise. Sometimes it's best to tie your request to your annual performance appraisal. A request for a raise is not unexpected then.

Other good times are when you've added new business, saved the company money, been asked to take on a new set of responsibilities, or had a stunning success. The one thing you don't want to do is sandbag the boss. If you're asking for more money at an unexpected time, let her know in advance. Yes, that does give her more time to prepare her objections, but it also gives her more time to review your performance and consider the reasons that you *should* get more money.

Prove your worth. As you carry out your daily duties, keep a record of the contributions you've made to the bottom line. For example, you could say, "I wrote seventeen stories for company publications. You normally would have farmed those stories out to freelancers and paid at least five hundred dollars for each one, so my extra work saved the company a minimum of nearly nine thousand dollars. I'd like to be considered for a portion of those savings."

Or, "I brought in two new accounts this year, each one worth close to a half-million dollars, which is twice as much as the financial target we set, and I think it's fair that I be rewarded for the business I developed." Or, "When Emily left the company, I was asked to take on her duties temporarily. Because I streamlined procedures so well, we didn't have to replace her at all, so there was a savings in both salary and benefits. I think you'd agree that performance like that deserves some additional compensation."

In short, don't so much ask for a raise as for a portion of the money you have earned or saved the company. You've benefited them financially; it's time for them to reciprocate.

Do your research. What do other people in your industry make if they have experience similar to yours? Taking into account regional differences (salaries are generally lower in

Wichita than they are in New York City), are you at the bottom, middle, or top of the range? Your raise request must be reasonable, or your boss will either laugh or get annoyed. In either case, you'll go away empty-handed. Never attempt to negotiate without hard figures.

Widen your definition. What is a raise? It's more real dollars in your pocket, and there are various ways to get it. If there's no excess cash available beyond a cost-of-living increase, there may be cash-equivalent perks you can negotiate for.

If the company will upgrade all your home telecommuting equipment, those are purchases you don't have to make. A company car relieves you of a monthly payment as well as gasoline and maintenance expenses. More vacation equates to additional paid time off.

An extra training opportunity you don't have to pay for is cash you can use for something else and also a way to enhance your skills and improve your productivity for this or a future job. Sometimes you can ask for a bonus in lieu of a long-term raise. That's an attractive option if you think next year's performance might be less stellar than this year's.

Should you be able to get only part of what you need now, ask for another review in less than a year—perhaps in three to six more months—to negotiate for the rest. Sometimes *no* means only *not now.*

Be a professional. "I need the money" or "We're having another baby" or "I blew my bonus in Las Vegas" are not reasons for which the company should give you a raise. A raise is a reward for productivity, not something the company provides because you're having a hard time making ends meet. Leave your personal reasons for wanting more money at the door and negotiate from a position of strength.

If you must have more money and you can't earn it where you work now, look around for other opportunities, but don't make idle threats about leaving if you don't get your raise. The boss may then view you as a short-timer and begin seeking a replacement. Never say you'll quit unless you're ready to walk out the door that day.

When you think you deserve a raise, be positive, creative, flexible, and patient. Those attributes will greatly increase the chances for more jingle in your jeans, now and in the future.

What if the thing you want is a promotion? Watch how you ask for it. Don't say, "I've been in the same job for three years. I've learned all I can and I'm bored." Instead, begin your campaign for a promotion by proving you're capable of more. Seize initiative—volunteer for a special project. Take advantage of company training opportunities. Seek some additional duties.

Most important, look for openings you're prepared to fill. When the time is right, you can say, "In the past year, I've increased my value to the company by upgrading my skills, taking university-level courses in project management, and working on the new markets initiative. I'd like to continue my career with this company, and I think I can contribute more effectively in another position. I'd welcome the responsibility, and I've prepared myself to take on the duties." A statement like this highlights something beyond your own self-interest and is more likely to give you the result you want.

Perhaps what you want most of all is a transfer to a new department. Before you attempt to make a jump, consider why you want to leave your current environment. If it's because of personality conflicts, be aware that those types of clashes might occur in another department, too. Examine your own role in such conflicts. Can you modify your behavior and salvage the situation in your current position? Have you tried to work out differences with your boss or coworkers? Have you exhausted your options?

Make a game plan. You can't just rocket into someone's office and say you need to move to another department in the company—today. While you're trying to work things out in your current job, prepare yourself for the move you want to make. Sign up for training. Learn new skills and polish the old ones. Become familiar with people and operations in the department to which you want to move.

Have lunch with potential workmates in the new department and participate with them in company-wide events to gauge how comfortable you are with them. Then couch your transfer request in terms that show your concern for the company as well as for yourself:

"I've been in the finance department for a couple of years now, but I've found that my real interest is in marketing. I've been taking some courses in marketing functions, and I think my finance background brings an important dimension to marketing decisions. I like the creativity of marketing as opposed to the more traditional finance duties. There's a position opening in the marketing department that I'm qualified for, and I'd like to apply for it. I'll do everything I can do to help train a replacement here."

Don't mention the wretched atmosphere in the finance department or how miserable you are, particularly if you're talking to your boss. Keep it positive and don't burn bridges. If you stay in the company, you're sure to encounter former colleagues and your former boss. Your professionalism in seeking a transfer can keep these encounters upbeat and pleasant.

IN THE OFFICE: DEALING WITH MISUNDERSTANDINGS AND DIFFICULT COWORKERS

Because we often spend as much time (or more) with coworkers as we do with family members, it's not surprising that we can have the same kinds of issues with them as we do at home. Misunderstandings and personality conflicts are common in all kinds of work settings, and letting issues percolate without resolution can lead to strained relationships, unproductive teams, and less-than-stellar results.

The keys to settling workplace disputes are the same, no matter what the problem: a coworker's taking credit for your work, using your computer inappropriately, creating noise pollution in a cubicle farm, denigrating your work to others, or lying about you.

First, gather the facts. When settling a dispute, it's always best to proceed on a factual basis, not from supposition and half-truths.

Keep your opinions, suspicions, and irritation to yourself. It's not necessary to involve the entire workplace in your issues with someone else. Don't blab to your coworkers or run to the boss. Start at the bottom, with the person who's bugging you; if you can't work it out, there's still time to bring in reinforcements. There's no need to use a howitzer to swat a housefly.

Approach your coworker in person. E-mail is the coward's way out, and there's far too much opportunity for misunderstanding in an e-mail. The tone and meaning can be misconstrued, and if the other person takes your message amiss, the stage is set for an exchange of incendiary charges and countercharges that lead to further anger and an ugly impasse.

Approach your coworker politely. Accusations and hot words rarely accomplish anything. State your issue and how you'd like it resolved. It might sound like this: "Jerry, I noticed that Sam gave you a lot of credit in the meeting for the report you and I wrote together. You deserve that credit because the writing was brilliant. However, I designed the matrix for the results, created all the charts and figures, and edited the entire thing. I was disappointed when you didn't pass some of the credit my way."

Listen to the response. When you close down your preconceptions and really listen, you may hear some surprising things:

1. "Sarah, you're right. I'll send an e-mail to Sam right away with a copy to you."
2. "Sarah, maybe I did take more credit than I should have, but I had to spend the entire night before the deadline redoing all the graphs. You miscopied one of my figures and it threw all the calculations off, and I didn't discover the problem until you had given me back your edited copy. You didn't find the mistake in your edit, and if I hadn't gone over it again, I would have looked ridiculous. I was exhausted from being up all night, and I guess I wasn't in the mood to say nice

things about your part. Maybe I was too hasty because that matrix was terrific. I can put that part in an e-mail to Sam and be telling the truth."

3. "Who do you think you are? That was my report and my work. I don't know why you think you deserve any credit."

4. "Sarah, you snooze, you lose. You should have spoken up. Protect yourself; don't expect me to do it. You screwed up—too bad."

Of course, Answer 1 is ideal, but you have to be open to the possibility that you might hear something else. Answer 2 is upsetting, but it explains why you probably won't get everything you want on this go-round. Answers 3 and 4 are unfortunately the way some people look at the world, but at least the cards are on the table.

Ask yourself if this credit grab is important enough for you to notify management of your contributions. If the project was one of many of equal value, you might choose to take your medicine this time and understand that Jerry isn't someone you can trust in the future.

However, if the project was a major career-builder, you may have to send an e-mail to Sam yourself. Your e-mail should not indicate that Jerry's a no-good rat; instead, you might include a copy of the matrix you designed, along with a detailed analysis of how you constructed it. Sam will understand what you're saying, and you won't have burned a co-worker in the process. That's professional.

CONFRONTING THE BOSS

Occasionally the issue you have to address is with your boss. Maybe she negates every good idea you have; maybe she's curt and unfriendly; perhaps she doesn't give you clear directions. Or, more rarely, maybe she's just impossible.

In the last case, there may be little you can do except to

get out as fast as you can, but you can deal with other issues. Here's a little tip: bosses are people. They have families and dogs and hobbies and fears and anxieties. If you approach your boss professionally and reasonably, you'll usually get a reasonable response.

Suppose your boss is constantly negative. She seems to shoot down every suggestion you make, sometimes in front of others, and you're beginning to feel that you can never satisfy her. Before you confront her, envision the result you want, which is probably to create a different working relationship, and make sure your language will move you toward that result.

Ask for a meeting and be direct in your approach. Describe what happens when you offer an idea and how that makes you feel. Don't attack, and keep the focus on yourself rather than on her. Don't make assumptions about her motives for treating you the way she does. Just state the facts as you see them, and then listen. You might say, "Meredith, in the past few months, I've offered some suggestions about personnel reassignments and office procedures. None of my ideas have been considered, and in fact they've been rejected very quickly. I'm wondering why. I'm beginning to feel uncertain and tentative. I want to contribute, but I'm not sure I know the best way. Can you help me understand what I might do differently?"

Now, close your mouth and open your ears. Her answer might be, "Your ideas are generally not bad, but you don't think them through to the end. You don't always consider how your suggestions affect other people. I'd encourage you to do more thorough analysis. Look at things from different perspectives, not just your own. You're smart, and if you stop going off half-cocked, you'll get a better response from me."

Or the answer might be, "You have great ideas, but you're too timid. I shoot back at you because I want you to toughen up, take a stand, and defend what you think is right to do. But you back down every time. It's disappointing because you're talented."

Or, "Really? It's never been my intention to intimidate you or make you feel less valuable. I do listen to you, and I don't think it's accurate to say that I've rejected *every* idea. I thought your suggestions for the telecommuting associates were very helpful, and I acted on them. Maybe I should have given you more credit for that, or at least told you that your contribution was helpful and sound. I'm under so much pressure that I don't always give enough pats on the back, and I apologize for that. I need your ideas, so keep them coming. I'll try to be more appreciative in the future."

Any one of these answers points you toward your desired result. You *can* be more analytical. You *can* advocate for your ideas more strongly. You *can* realize that you might have taken a few rejections too personally. All those actions probably will result in a better relationship.

However, you might also hear, "You're right. I don't think you have very good ideas, and I'm disappointed in your performance most of the time." There can be no clearer message than that. Quietly begin a job search elsewhere. You're going nowhere with this company.

Whatever the outcome, straight-from-the-shoulder, nonjudgmental communication is very powerful. Don't be afraid of it.

IN THE OFFICE: DEALING WITH SENSITIVE ISSUES

As medical science advances, there will be times when coworkers may be diagnosed with illnesses ranging from Parkinson's disease to autoimmune conditions to various kinds of cancer. Sometimes a colleague may continue on the job right through radiation and chemotherapy, and his appearance and level of stamina may change radically during the course of therapy.

Knowing what to say in these situations may be difficult. People who have survived life-threatening illness often remark that they have been bemused and nonplussed—and sometimes deeply hurt—by the heartless, careless statements people have made to them. For example, it's not unusual to hear:

- "Oh, my mother had breast cancer, too. The treatment was so terrible she had to stop, and then she died."
- "Well, you've always put yourself under too much stress, and you know there's a connection between stress and cancer. I guess your body's trying to tell you something."
- "You're going to be just fine. Buck up and keep a positive attitude."
- "How much time do you think you'll miss? I can't do my work and yours for very long or I'll just collapse."

When a coworker tells you she's ill, find out if she has told others as well. If you are the only one who knows, you have a duty to your colleague not to bandy the information about. She may have good reason for confiding only in you. Although many employers are supportive and kind to associates who are ill, there are others who will do nearly anything to get rid of someone fighting an illness, even if their tactics are illegal. People can be out of a job just when they need it most.

Once you know the situation, the best thing to say may be, "I'm sorry to hear you have to go through this. What are the most helpful things I can do for you while you're in treatment? Do you need help with any projects? Should I call you with updates when you can't be here? Would you like to be excused from meetings for a while? " These types of questions allow the person to be honest about what she needs.

When your colleague is well enough to be in the office, follow her lead about whether to talk about her illness. Work may be a refuge for her, the one place she can distract herself with meaningful tasks. Don't invade that space by insisting on knowing all the details of treatment or what the latest tests have shown. When she wants you to know, she'll tell you. "How's it going today?" will allow her to share what she wishes and maintain privacy about what she wants to keep to herself.

Should she need to talk at length, try to make yourself available even if you find such conversations uncomfortable; getting a coworker through a rough patch is worth a little discomfort. If you find yourself over your head, however, you might suggest a support group or a therapist to deal with medical questions or social issues. A group of people who've been through it can provide comfort, offer a dose of reality, and even find dark humor in the midst of some pretty grim circumstances. However, humor isn't something *you* should attempt; leave that to your colleague's support group.

Many other types of personal situations can have an impact on the workplace. There will be times when coworkers, managers, or top brass will experience a family crisis, and you must respond to the situation appropriately. Tragedy has a way of either making people tongue tied or causing them to say things that are remarkably gauche. A pregnant woman who has miscarried doesn't need to be told that she can have other children or that it's "good it happened now before you got too attached to the baby." A mother is attached to her child from the moment she knows she's carrying it, and to say otherwise is immeasurably insensitive.

Most of the time, people misspeak because they don't know what to say and end up blurting out the first thing that pops into their brain. On the other hand, they may try to cheer up the person in crisis, which often has the effect of trivializing his pain or grief.

There is a quality that, if exercised, keeps us from making the kinds of statements that embarrass us and cause pain for others. That quality is empathy. Empathy is not sympathy, although the words are somewhat related. Empathy is the ability to feel *with* other people and to fully experience what they're going through. An empathetic person steps into the other's shoes and says what he would like to hear if the situation were reversed. A person blessed with empathy finds that the right words flow easily.

When a coworker's family member dies, the empathetic response may be only a few words, such as, "We are so sorry for your loss," or "I know this time has been so difficult for you, and I've admired how beautifully you saw to your father's needs." That has a far different ring from, "Your father was sick for such a long time; I know how hard it was, and you must be so relieved it's finally over." That's just offensive, but it's the kind of thing people often say when they don't think.

What people in grief don't need is unspecified offers of help. "Just let us know if there's anything you want" is a meaningless phrase. It's far better to offer concrete assistance. You can choose what to do by observing what needs to be done. For example, perhaps a coworker's child has become gravely ill. He is racked with worry but is also concerned about a looming deadline. "I know you've been anxious about keeping the Patterson proposal on track. I'll gather the figures for the last three quarters and summarize the trends. They'll be on your desk when you come back to the office." This help says far more and means far more than vague platitudes.

In a crisis, an offer like this, if it's backed up by real action, relieves the other person of the tyranny of details, and it's emphatically the right thing to say.

Be an office star:

- Focus on your job
- Keep your communication clear, positive, and nonjudgmental
- Maintain a professional attitude, even in unpleasant circumstances
- Deal sensitively and courteously with everyone in the company, from the CEO to the cafeteria staff
- Listen at least as much as you talk

10

SOUNDING SMART IN PUBLIC

SPEECHES, PANELS, AND MEDIA APPEARANCES

THE SPEECH PEOPLE REMEMBER

You may never be an international motivational speaker, scurrying around a stage screaming into your headset and basking in the adulation of thousands of rapt disciples, but that's not all there is to speeches. From making a toast to introducing a seminar leader to conducting a sales meeting to being a keynote speaker, you're on stage far more often than you might imagine. Do it right and you'll cement your reputation as a professional; do it wrong and your audience starts measuring you for cement shoes.

A speaking engagement positions you as someone with more knowledge than the average person about a particular topic. The audience will view you as a specialist, and that's a good position to be in. As you give more speeches, keep a log of where you appeared and what your topics were. Also keep copies of your audience evaluations. Your boss may not know you're a speaker, and if you're receiving excellent evaluations at your appearances, it's something you'll want to mention.

Although speaking engagements may not directly affect your daily work, you can talk about them at your performance appraisal as proof of your commitment to developing all aspects of your career and bringing additional positive attention to your company. Moreover, the very fact that you're being invited to give speeches—and not on company time—makes you someone to watch.

Before you even begin the process of preparing a presentation, learn everything you can about the purpose of your talk and those who will attend. Audience knowledge is essential. Everything you do and say—from the words you choose to the clothes you wear—is based on who's in the seats. You need to know:

- The purpose of the speech
- The audience demographics: age, sex, and occupation, at the very least
- The size of the audience
- Whether audience attendance is voluntary or required
- Where and when the speech will be held
- The length of time you're to speak
- Whether you are the only speaker or one of many; where you fall in the program

DOWN TO BUSINESS

As you write your speech, remember this: Your presentation is not for you. It's for the audience. If your audience can't make the connection between your talk and their experience, the speech will flop. As you write each point, picture your audience asking, "So what? How does that affect me?" A presentation is not the place for self-indulgence. Get out of your own way and concentrate all your efforts on the needs and expectations of the audience.

Every speech, no matter how elementary or complex, is a three-act play: Act 1 is the beginning, Act 2 is the middle—the meaty part of your talk—and Act 3 is the end. Each act has a different function, but all must be strong and polished if your presentation is to stick in people's minds.

Opening Your Presentation

The beginning of a presentation is tricky. Let's say you've been asked to make a presentation on hiring older Americans. The central point of your talk is that older workers make great employees and that negative perceptions about them are unfounded. Your opening must grab the audience by the scruff of the neck and make them care about your topic, and you have about one minute, perhaps ten sentences, to do that. Yet every day, hundreds—maybe even thousands—of speakers ignore the importance of the opening, falling back on stale, trite formulas and dooming their presentations from the beginning. Here are some of the most ineffective openings:

The rhetorical question opening. "Have you ever wondered . . . ?" "Did you know that . . . ?" What if they haven't wondered? What if they don't care? The best way to spice up this opening is to write the answer and then ditch the question. Use the answer as your opening. "More than a million older Americans reenter the job market each year, and employers are overjoyed to welcome them back."

The "I'm happy to be here" opening. It's gracious to acknowledge your hosts, but a long-winded thank-you pulls focus from your topic. You may certainly acknowledge the person who introduces you, but it should be little more than, "Thank you, Matilda."

The definition opening. "Webster's Dictionary defines . . ." To turn Nike's slogan upside down, just *don't* do it. The definition opening is usually so dull that you can see the audience settling down for a nice long nap.

The quotation opening. If you can find a riveting, little-known quotation that's directly on point, go ahead and give it a shot. However, steer clear of clichés, platitudes, and quotations that have grown shopworn from overuse.

The "now that I have your attention" opening. You know

this one: "Sex, drugs, and rock and roll. Now that I have your attention, let's talk about hiring older Americans." The first time someone used this opening, it might have resulted in a laugh, but four billion repetitions later, it's just annoying. It has nothing to do with the topic, almost always contains some inappropriate sexual innuendo, and makes it hard for you to gain audience trust. You've cheated them once and they wonder if you're going to do it again.

The joke opening. A great joke that's well told and illustrates the point of your talk can be an unforgettable opening. It's chancy, though—nerves can play havoc with your memory. You might leave out an important point ("Oh, wait, I forgot. He's ninety-eight years old!") or blow the punch line. Stage fright can ruin your tempo and timing.

The biggest reason for not using jokes is that joke telling is an art most of us haven't perfected. There are those rare people who were born with an understanding of beat, rhythm, and emphasis, but most of us weren't. Moreover, not everyone finds the same things amusing. It's best to opt for an opening that doesn't offer such a high risk of failure.

Openings That Work

Real questions that require audience participation. "How many of you would hire a retiree who wants to return to the work force?"

Grabber statistics. "I'm going to be speaking for twenty minutes. From now until the time I sit down, four hundred older Americans will have lost their jobs, their benefits, and their hope. And the workforce will have lost a priceless resource."

A twist. "I'm sixty-five years old, and I'm supposed to talk with you about retirement. I can't; I've just gone back to work."

A story. "Last year, my sixty-three-year-old mother went back to work. After putting in thirty years at her previous job, she retired, but she hated the boredom and the golf. She said she'd lost her purpose. I thought her age would work against her in finding another job, but she was snapped up at her first interview. Apparently, she's in the vanguard of a new movement."

After the Opening

The middle of your presentation contains all the examples, anecdotes, data, and details that support your one-sentence main thesis: that older workers make great employees. You may have to research heaps of articles or interview several people to glean all the information and illustrative stories you need to make your presentation sing, but then you're ready to write. How you organize the material is up to you, but an easy-to-follow, straightforward approach works best for most topics. Lay out a problem and show the audience how and why your solution works and benefits them.

Quick Tip: Writing for the Ear

Remember that writing a speech is different from writing an article. To deliver the most effective speeches, bear the following points in mind:

- Keep your style conversational, but don't be careless. Check for grammatical errors, misplaced modifiers, and other mistakes that will detract from your message.
- Use short, punchy sentences that the audience can follow without working too hard.
- Choose simple yet evocative words that make it easy for your audience to picture what you're talking about.
- Use the active voice to keep momentum going.
- Spend some time working on inventive comparisons so you don't have to fall back on clichés such as *busy as a beaver* or *light as a feather*.

Attack your subject from various angles. Explain that older Americans' work ethic has a beneficial effect on younger workers; talk about older workers' commitment to customer service; let the audience know that the technology gap between older and younger workers is closing; emphasize older workers' superior problem-solving skills, honed by years of experience; show that productivity does not decline simply because someone has gotten older. Mix statistical data and quotations from experts, which offer credibility, with anecdotal information, which humanizes and warms up your presentation.

Closing the Presentation

Once you've made your points, close brilliantly. Your first impression is long gone and the last impression is what your audience will take home with them. Avoid:

The just-messing-with-your-head close. The end that never ends. The speaker says, "In conclusion . . . ," and then proceeds to drone on, maybe adding new information or reiterating previously made points in a continuous, interminable loop. This type of close makes the audience both restless and resentful.

The rundown close. Speakers who use this close look and sound as if they've suddenly grown tired of their own presentation. They may tap their notes on the lectern, stare at them for a moment, and then pull out some feeble final statement: "Well, I guess I don't have any more to say," or, "That's the end of my remarks." The audience is let down and confused, and the speaker wonders why no one has any questions.

The oh-my-gosh-look-at-the time close. The speaker has run over the time allotted for the presentation, tries to cram the few last points into a very few minutes and winds up with, "Sorry to have kept you so long." Guess what? The audience is sorry, too, because they've been delayed by someone who didn't think their time was valuable. That's just rude.

Close your presentation by tying the end to the beginning; the last thing out of your mouth should be the one idea you want your audience to remember. "If you have a job to give, consider an older worker. You'll get loyalty, skill, and experience, and that's a winning combination." Then thank the audience and either leave the stage to window-rattling applause or indicate you'll be happy to take some questions.

Visual Aids: The Speaker's Friend?

Think of the great presenters you've seen. How many of them depended on visual aids?

Abraham Lincoln put his notes for the Gettysburg Address on the back of an envelope or on the cuff of his shirt, depending on which account you accept—and both of them are wrong. A meticulous speechwriter, Lincoln actually worked on the address at the White House before traveling to Pennsylvania. Wherever he wrote his notes, however, you can be sure that Lincoln didn't project those jottings on a massive screen. Martin Luther King Jr.'s "I Have a Dream" speech was presented with no more than a lectern and a microphone—and yet the whole world stopped to listen.

The purpose of visual aids is to help your audience remember key points. Your job is to present, explain, and expand on those points: to persuade, inform, create understanding, build consensus, generate questions, and fire up discussion—in short, to make a presentation.

Today, some speakers believe you can't make a speech without using PowerPoint. According to Dave Paradi, author of *Guide to PowerPoint* (Prentice Hall, 2006), approximately thirty million PowerPoint business presentations are given every day in the United States and a huge percentage of them are poorly researched, badly constructed, and excruciatingly delivered. These results can be traced to misunderstanding and misuse of technology.

PowerPoint is quick, easy, and fun. Those very qualities make it seductive. Because they can create good-looking slides quickly and easily, speakers may depend too much on technology at the expense of preparation and practice; and because they also have access to animation, presenters are far too inclined to experiment with fly-ins, fades, spins, zooms, dissolves, flashbulbs, and wipes, all of which, if overused, can detract from their message and leave the audience dazed and dizzy.

Although PowerPoint is an excellent resource for creating colorful charts and graphs, it's less effective for conveying text. Slides should contain no more than six words per line and no more than two to three lines. If there's a lot of ground to cover, you may have to create an epic-length slide show, and that defeats the purpose of your presentation. It eliminates all the factors—body language, eye contact, and vocal variety—that establish a bond between the presenter and the audience, make a speech riveting, and build a speaker's reputation as an expert.

The biggest mistake you can make is to put your entire speech on slides and then read them to your audience. When you stand in front of a group and recite your slides, you snub the audience by turning your back on them; make it harder for attendees to hear you, which makes it more likely they'll misunderstand what you say; prevent your listeners from engaging with you and your subject matter, which shuts down opportunities for later discussion; and guarantee that everyone in the audience will be bored and inattentive.

Rather than make the slides your centerpiece, it's best not to call attention to them at all. A business theater event producer for whom I sometimes write scripts and speeches says,

> Don't interrupt the flow of your speech by turning to your graphic and saying, "As you can see on the slide . . ." Once you do that, you've directed the audience's attention away from you and your message to the slide itself, and you'll have to work to get them to refocus. Let the graphics speak for themselves.
>
> I tell speakers who are using slides to steer clear of the word *as* because it almost always means that they're going to turn to the slide and lose the audience: "as this chart demonstrates . . ."; "as you'll notice on this slide . . ."; "as you look at this graph . . ." It's much better to keep the audience looking at you all the time.

Visual aids are only an adjunct to your words, passion, personal power, and expertise. What makes your presentation special is not fancy graphics, but you. The elements that great speeches have in common are extensive preparation, hours of practice, a complete understanding of both the purpose of the speech and what the audience needs to hear, and meticulous attention to constructing the rhythm of the words themselves. Thinking about the substance of your remarks and delivering them succinctly may make visual aids unnecessary.

Quick Tip: Timing Is Everything

If you've prepared handouts for your audience, hold the notes for distribution until after you've finished your speech. Otherwise, audience members will be reading while you're presenting, and they'll miss important information or supporting details you haven't included in the handout.

On Your Mark: Practice

With all the tasks clamoring for your time, you may be tempted to skimp on practicing your speech. Don't succumb to the temptation. Not practicing your presentation means a substandard performance, and giving that kind of lackluster effort when you're capable of more is insulting to your audience. You owe them your best; practice is essential.

Practice involves a variety of dimensions. On the first run-through, see whether the presentation fits within the time frame you've been assigned, and trim or augment your remarks accordingly. Practice a few more times in front of a mirror to observe your posture and gestures as you become more familiar with your material. Once you know where your speech is going:

Make an audio recording of yourself. An audio recording will point out poor organization; weak transitions; lazy enunciation; a pace that is too rapid; colorless, flat delivery; a squeaky pitch; and the bugaboo of many speakers, vocalized pauses.

A nonvocalized pause, which is a second or two of silence, can be a powerful way to set off and emphasize key ideas. A vocalized pause—"er, uh, ya know, right?" or "OK?"—detracts from your message; your audience starts keeping score of how many times you interrupt yourself instead of listening to what you have to say. These verbal tics may lessen as you become more comfortable with your presentation, but be on the lookout for them throughout your preparation.

Videotape your speech. Watch the tape with the sound on and then with the sound off. During the first viewing, look for congruence between what you say and how you say it. Is your voice monotonous or singsong? Do you pause and slow down appropriately when you're making a major point, or do you gloss over important features by not altering your rate or adjusting your style? During the second viewing, eliminate the sound and concentrate on your posture, the appropriateness of your gestures, and the amount of eye contact you make with the audience.

Your gestures should amplify the important points you make, not distract from them. Gestures should not be repetitious; some speakers chop the air with every sentence or make the same gesture to emphasize every point. Build your talk so that your gestures flow naturally from your words. "On the one hand . . . and on the other" invites a specific gesture. A gesture that crosses your body can look both awkward and threatening, as if you're getting ready to backhand the audience; an open-handed gesture can invite audience participation. You can use very forceful gestures, such as striking your palm with your fist, as long as you don't direct such gestures at the audience.

When you feel you're ready, practice in front of a live audience composed of business colleagues or honest friends. You might ask one to critique your choice of words, another to listen for *ers* and *ums*, and another to make comments on your gestures and physical presence.

Revise your notes. In the world of speeches and presentations, there are two extremes, both of which have positives and negatives. On the one hand are the speakers who read their speeches. This presentation style ensures that the speaker won't leave out any critical information. The downside is that speech readers often don't lift their heads from the printed page. The audience might not be sure what the speaker looks like, but they're quite familiar with his bald spot or the fact that her roots need to be touched up.

At the other end of the spectrum are the presenters who memorize their talks, and these people can be very effective speakers. With the words committed to memory, the presenter is free to concentrate on delivery and drama. However, without attention and polishing, a memorized speech can sound mechanistic and flavorless.

For most speakers, taking the middle ground is the best course. When you know your presentation well, cut your notes down to a few key words. Put those on note cards in great big type you can read without squinting if you misplace your glasses. Put the cards on the lectern and refer to them only if you need them.

Get Set . . .

Don't believe that once you've written and polished your speech, all you have to do is show up and deliver it. You also need to know about where you'll be speaking. Will you be in a dining nook or a conference room? Will a large area be divided with a temporary wall so that the sound of another presentation may bleed into yours? Will people be clearing dishes when you're speaking? What adjustments will you have to make to handle such factors?

Practice with the microphone for a few minutes before your audience appears. If you've brought slides, test the projection equipment to see that everything can be connected.

In short, try to anticipate anything that could detract from your performance and do what you can to control it. The last thing you must do before you step onto the stage is turn off your cell phone. You're not going to answer it if it rings, so there's no need to have it on.

Go!

What audiences are looking for when they come to hear a speaker is *presence*, which is a hard concept to define. During an *Inside the Actors Studio* interview, actress Glenn Close discussed how certain performers "disturb the air," and that's what best describes presence. Once you walk out to speak, the atmosphere should be different from what it was before you were introduced. Whatever your speaking style—reserved and elegant or bodacious and boisterous—it must convey certainty, confidence, and an eagerness to share your area of expertise.

You can express these attributes best through an easy but not sloppy posture; a pleasant yet audible tone; welcoming, natural gestures; constant eye contact with your entire audience, not just the folks in the front; clear, colorful language that helps your audience see what you're talking about; and an obvious passion for your subject, even if that subject is a juiceless financial report. You have to care about what those figures mean if you want anyone else to.

Very few people are born with these abilities. You develop them over time through long hours of practice. Toastmasters International, which has chapters all over the world, is a good forum for learning how to communicate effectively on the platform or in meetings. Many excellent speakers got their start at Toastmasters, and many already good speakers have honed their skills there.

Special Issue 1: Stage Fright

A little stage fright—a few flutters in the stomach—is not a bad thing. It helps you stay alert and sharpens your performance. It means you care about what you're going to say and want to do a good job.

However, for some people, stage fright is more than momentary shakiness. It's an overwhelming bodily reaction to the feeling of being trapped in a stressful situation. When the body senses it's in danger, it adapts by engaging its fight-orflight response, an exquisitely honed mechanism that has ensured human survival across the millennia.

The problem is that the body may be doing more for us than we need. Giving a speech is not the same kind of stress our prehistoric ancestors faced when they were dashing away from a wooly mammoth. Effective survival mechanisms die hard, however, and the more you perceive speaking in public as a danger, the more your body will try to help out.

After you've given many speeches, paralyzing stage fright is usually replaced by a manageable kind of anticipatory excitement. Until that day comes, here are a few good hints for eliminating or at least lessening the effects of stage fright:

Imagine your audience enjoying the presentation. Think of them as fellow sojourners, not harsh critics. It's not necessary to visualize them naked or in their underwear; just consider them friends.

Know your beginning, know your ending, and know your stuff. Having your opening committed to memory gets you past the first moment of fear. Once you're through that part, inertia takes over—you're in motion and you tend to stay in motion. Memorizing your close helps you finish strongly and confidently, and knowing your stuff means that even if you wander from your prepared text or your notes get scrambled, you'll still be able to make all your important points.

Take a beat between being introduced and beginning your talk. A brief pause gives everyone a moment to make the transition from activity to listening. Smile at the audience as they settle down; it relaxes your face.

Ease cotton mouth by taking a sip of water. Don't guzzle the whole glass; just wet your lips and begin your talk.

Remember that this too shall pass. As you enter fully into the event, your nerves will diminish. That's the thing about stage fright: once you're on the stage, it ebbs or disappears, and you can begin to enjoy the experience.

Special Issue 2: The Hostile Audience

In very few cases does an audience actively dislike a speaker, but they may not be happy about the speaker's message. Nonetheless, someone has to deliver hard news occasionally, and the best result a speaker can hope for is that the audience spares the messenger.

It's rare for speakers not to know they're walking into a tense situation. You're aware that if yours is an unpopular opinion about a potentially explosive issue, you may be in for a tough time.

If you find yourself in a hostile environment, it's wise to address major concerns at the outset: "I'm here to present an opinion some of you will agree with and some of you won't. I want you to know that I respect your right to disagree with me, and I'm going to listen as hard as I can to your concerns to see if there's anything I've overlooked that might help us find our way to common ground. I'm looking forward to an honest, productive exchange of views, and I hope we can each walk away at least somewhat satisfied with the outcome."

An opening statement like this accomplishes several important goals. It sets clear expectations for the meeting, and it also creates an atmosphere of civility. A speaker who is polite and considerate of others is likely to evoke a similar attitude in the audience. We usually get back what we put out, so speakers who are confrontational and caustic—the "my way or the highway" types—may very well have their heads handed to them by a resentful, resistant audience.

As you step through your presentation, you might discover that it's not the whole audience that's hostile but only a few vocal naysayers who like basking in the spotlight. They're often inconsiderate, loutish, loud, and obnoxious, and the rest of the audience is probably as uncomfortable as you are with the way these people behave. Dealing with hecklers and blowhards appropriately may help you win over the more-silent majority with your style alone. Here are some techniques that work:

Prepare for the issues that are likely to surface and have your answers and facts at hand. However, understand that audience members may have questions you haven't anticipated, which means you'll have to think on your feet.

Dump your preconceptions about what you believe a particular audience member's argument will be, and listen with attention to what he's really saying. Even in the midst of a diatribe, you might hear something that will help you defuse a tense situation.

Listen until the speaker is finished, and respond to the issue, not the attitude. Maintain eye contact and keep your body quiet, no matter how annoyed you may be. No clenching your fists or rolling your eyes, no heavy sighs, no hands on hips or arms crossed across the chest. Don't interrupt, jump in with justifications, ask for clarification, or begin a debate in the middle of the question. Hold on to your temper, and don't allow yourself to be baited into an ugly exchange.

Scan the room. Some experts advise that you should address only the person raising an objection; others believe it's best to give your answer to the entire audience. If you see lots of head nodding in agreement with the audience member, opt for the latter suggestion; if only the speaker appears to be agitated, maintain eye contact with him.

Pause before giving your answer. The speaker may have "just one more thing to say." Rushing to respond makes it seem as if you weren't really listening, and she'll probably interrupt you to finish making her points.

Answer only the question that's been asked. When someone in the audience asks you what time it is, don't tell him how to build a watch. The more you stray from the actual question, the more you invite further disagreement. Answer the question fully, but avoid digressing to peripheral topics.

Insist that the questioner maintain the same boundaries. If she starts to wander, say, "Right now, the issue we're discussing is pay concessions. I want to hear everyone's concerns about that before we move on to another subject."

Tell the truth. A lie will be found out eventually, and your credibility will be damaged, perhaps beyond repair.

Use inclusive language. A "we/you" dichotomy can prevent dialogue, but including the whole audience in the "we" may help to foster some unity of purpose.

Realize that a minority opinion may have considerable substance and truth to it. If yours is the majority position, don't dismiss the other's point of view just because the speaker is unpleasant and you're going to win anyway. Use what's true in his argument to try to find the middle ground.

Be careful with humor. You might believe that a light touch will tone down the rhetoric, but it's more likely the other person will feel ridiculed, and the audience may turn further against you.

Compromise if you can, but don't hold out hope of conciliation if you have no intention of changing your position. Appearing flexible when you aren't is dishonest, and sometimes the facts are the facts and there's nothing you or anyone else can do to change them.

Don't allow yourself to be kicked around. When another's words become threatening, you have a perfect right to close him down by calling on someone else. If you know in advance that a gathering has the potential to go beyond your control and become explosive, think about meeting with smaller groups at different times so the hotheads have a smaller audience. And if you believe the situation actually might become violent, make sure there's adequate, visible security in the meeting room.

Psychologists tell us that anger is always the second emotion. The first, which may precede anger by only a nanosecond, is often an unmet expectation, frustration, disappointment, fear, or embarrassment. By listening carefully to those who are asking questions, you may be able to identify the real feeling behind the hostility. Once you isolate and address the initial emotion, you can often put out the fire quickly.

Several years ago, when I was in my office at the hospital, I received an irate phone call from a man whose wife had died at one of the system's facilities. He said, "I can't understand why you'd be sending her a letter asking for a contribution to your foundation. For God's sake, she died in your hospital! Don't you keep track? I didn't need this today." His anger was feeding on itself and he was becoming more and more upset.

I think he was expecting me to provide an alibi: to tell him that the hospital was big and our department didn't have access to all the patient records. I think he expected to hear about clerical errors. But what I said was, "Mr. Jones, I'm so sorry. This is an inexcusable error. It happened to me, too, when my father died, and it upset me a great deal. I was in so much pain about losing him, and letters addressed to him made me feel that nobody cared. I will personally go over to the foundation office right now and have your wife's name removed from the mailing list, and please accept my condolences on your loss. Is there anything else you'd like to tell me or that I can do for you?"

The change in his attitude was nearly instantaneous. By speaking to his grief rather than his anger, I was able to help him regain his composure. He thanked me courteously for listening to him and for taking care of his complaint. This technique can work with larger audiences, too.

Special Issue 3: Questions You Can't Answer

The last part of many speeches is a question-and-answer period. Many speakers dread Q & A because they fear they'll be unmasked as frauds if they don't have an answer to every question any member of the audience can conjure up. Not true. There's a whole host of ways to deal with this eventuality, and not one of them hurts your credibility. First, make good eye contact and buy yourself a little time by repeating the question; if you can't come up with anything after that, you can use one of the following:

- "That's an excellent question, and I don't have an answer. I can research it for you and get back to you. I'd like to take your card after the session and send you the answer when I have it." (Don't forget to follow up with the answer in a few days.)

- "I have a partial answer to that question, but I'd like to throw the discussion open to everyone here. You know the specifics of your industry better than I do. Perhaps you can bring an insider's perspective I don't have."
- "I don't have an answer that's as specific as your question, but I can tell you what's true in similar cases."
- "Wow! Great question. I've never even considered that. Congratulations for stumping me. But believe me, I'll be thinking a lot about what you asked before I give this presentation again."

Stuff Happens

Even if you've completed the most extensive preparation on earth, you cannot be ready for anything—and anything is what might happen.

At a scientific presentation at a conference center in Tennessee, the speaker stepped to the lectern just as the exterminator arrived and started fogging the room where the meeting was being held. The presenter tried to say something witty, but she was choking on chemicals and couldn't get a word out. The event planner who told me this story swung into action, shooed the exterminator out, opened all the windows, sent the attendees to the lobby for a coffee break, rearranged the schedule to give the speaker and audience time to regroup, and kept everything moving with minimal damage to the day's activities.

A less happy outcome occurred at a meeting in Arizona. The committee chairperson had asked the breakfast plenary speaker, a colleague of mine, to prepare a forty-minute presentation. The speaker assigned the task to her associate, who delivered a speech that worked within the time frame and allowed fifteen minutes for questions and answers.

Unfortunately, the meal dragged on and the program committee members were not watching the time. When the speaker rose to give her talk, she had only fifteen minutes for her entire presentation. She hadn't prepared for that and was at a loss as to how to shorten her speech. Even though she dropped the question-and-answer period, she had lost 40 percent of her actual presentation time. She explained her feelings about the situation:

> It was disheartening. People kept getting up and walking out, not one or two at a time, but whole tables. I knew they had to; there were sessions that they didn't want to be late for, but it was embarrassing. Out of an audience of a few hundred, I ended up with about forty people in the room.
>
> I used the whole thing as a learning experience, and since that time, I've studied my presentations more carefully. I now mark sections I can cut without losing the power of the speech. I practice longer and shorter versions to make sure the transitions work if I have to cut. I'm much more ready for every contingency. That experience taught me that everything doesn't always go like clockwork, and presenters have to be flexible.

Public speaking doesn't have to be like tiptoeing through a war zone. It can be great fun if your preparation is exacting, your expectations reasonable, and your focus always outward. When you see audience members nodding their heads in agreement, you know you've connected with them; they're listening, and they're looking to you as someone who has something important to say. The rush of satisfaction you feel eliminates fear and makes speaking in public a pleasure.

ANOTHER KIND OF SPEAKING ENGAGEMENT: THE PANEL

A panel is an effective way to give an audience a great deal of information and a variety of viewpoints in a short period of time. Like giving a presentation, speaking on a panel can be an important career move. As a panelist, you have high visibility, and simply by virtue of your presence on the panel with other experts, you gain instant credibility. Audience members assume you're also an expert, or you wouldn't have been invited to participate.

Panels also give you the opportunity to meet other people in your company or field who may become your friends and even be helpful to you in advancing your career. It's too bad that many speakers are unaware of the value and cachet of panel membership and squander the opportunity by being unprepared, confrontational, self-important, or impolite. If you want to be the panelist or moderator everyone loves to hear, there are some important lessons to learn.

Before the Panel

Being on a panel is just like giving a presentation; the only difference is that other presenters share the stage with you. You are not solely responsible for the content of the presentation, which is often a relief. However, you must prepare your portion as carefully as if you were going to be alone on the podium. Just showing up and winging it is disrespectful as well as foolish. The other panelists probably will be well prepared, and you'll look like a bumbling amateur. If you know you don't have time to prepare properly for panel participation, decline the invitation with thanks, and try to keep the door open for a later opportunity.

Before you decide whether to take part, ask the same types of questions you would if you were making a solo speech: Who's the audience? What's the purpose of the panel? Who are the other panelists? How long will the panel speak, and how long should your specific presentation be? Will there be a question-and-answer period? Should you prepare handouts or other visual aids?

Once you know who's on the panel, it's a nice gesture to call or e-mail the other panelists. It's also a way to plan a strategy for everyone's participation. Talking with your copanelists and being active in helping to make the panel effective is the mark of a professional; those who are planning the meeting will appreciate your enterprising attitude, as will the other panelists.

Not long ago, I was one of two editorial consultants on a panel, which could have resulted in our presentations being repetitive. However, when we talked by e-mail a few weeks before the event, we decided that I would handle very practical aspects of the topic, while the other consultant would speak more generally about industry trends. We ended up with a well-rounded look at the entire subject instead of simply reiterating one another's information.

At the Event

Listen to the other panelists. It's bad form to look bored or uninterested until it's your turn to speak. The others on the panel are your equals in ability, and by listening to them you sometimes can learn as much as the audience. You also can incorporate some of their views into your answers if questions are directed to you during the open portion of the panel.

Using a lead-in such as "As Annmarie (or Dr. Expert) mentioned . . ." shares credit and shows respect for your copanelists. Should you disagree with another panelist's opinion, you can say so, cordially stating your points of divergence. Even if you disagree, quoting another speaker shows you've been paying attention, and that's the sign of a professional.

Don't hog the show. If you're allotted five minutes for your introductory remarks, don't take ten. Grabbing more than your assigned portion forces panelists who are more considerate of the time constraints to reorganize and shorten their presentations on the spot. That kind of thoughtlessness is annoying not only to your fellow speakers but also to the moderator and the audience. When the moderator is forced to cut you off—and a good one will—it's uncomfortable for everyone and mortifying for you.

Hold your tongue when it's appropriate. You don't need to put your two cents' worth in just to say you agree with another panelist's views. Give the other person his place in the sun. It's best to report by exception; that is, when the moderator allows the entire panel to speak to an issue, place your emphasis on what the other panelists *haven't* said. Of course, you may preface your comments by briefly stating points of agreement, but move quickly to your unique contribution.

Speak simply and directly. If the panel is a one-company or one-industry affair, you may be understood if you resort to jargon. However, there may be others in the audience, such as reporters, who aren't as familiar with in-speak, so avoid buzz-words and unnecessary complexity if you can. The harder a topic is to understand, the more you need to use colorful examples, specific illustrations, and precise language.

Questions and Answers

Some panels include brief opening statements from each panelist and perhaps a general question from the moderator. The rest of the session is questions and answers. This type of panel works well for introducing a new product, sharing specifications and directions, and presenting "how-to" topics.

For example, would-be authors who come to a writers' conference panel of agents and editors are brimming over with all sorts of practical questions: How do I get an agent? How long should I wait to hear back from an agent to whom I've submitted a manuscript or proposal? What's the typical advance for a first novel? If I've been rejected twenty-two times, should I give up? The panel has the answers and it behooves the moderator to get to the point—and to the Q & A—very quickly.

Other panels offer more time for individual presentations and fewer minutes for questions and answers. These panels work well for presenting research results or complex topics.

Whatever the panel type, when a question is directed to you, answer it as fully as you can, but feel free to pass it on to other panelists if there are aspects of the question that they can handle more authoritatively. Providing the greatest help you can, even if it means sharing the spotlight for a few minutes, is a courteous thing to do.

Extend that courtesy to audience members as well. No matter how many times you've answered the same question on other panels, it's not necessary to look impatient and sigh. It takes courage to ask a question of an expert, so be sensitive of others' feelings. Kindness is always the best policy; you don't want to be remembered for being a supercilious twit or a bully. That's bad for you and reflects very poorly on your company as well.

When possible, make yourself available for questions after the panel. Some people are too shy to ask a question in front of a room full of people. Others want to share insights or probe an issue in greater depth than is possible during a question-and-answer session. You enhance your reputation by being accessible to members of the audience, all of whom will remember your helpfulness and perhaps recommend you for other name-building engagements—or perhaps a future job. You never know who might be in the audience, so treat everyone as if she is the most important person in the world to you—because she could be.

Moderating the Event

If you've been named panel moderator, you have a lot to do. Upon arriving at the venue, your first tasks are to check in with the event coordinator and to look at the site where the panel will take place. Have microphones been delivered and set up? Has the room been made accessible for those with disabilities? If a sign language interpreter was requested, will she be on the premises at the required time?

Get comfortable with the audiovisual equipment; it's the mark of an amateur to begin the panel by tapping the microphone and asking the audience if the thing is working. Once you're satisfied with the room, it's off to a quiet location to meet with the panelists.

Introduce yourself and introduce copanelists to each other if they aren't already acquainted. This is the time to check pronunciation of names. Names are important to people, and they want them pronounced properly.

I once had to introduce a speaker with a four-syllable name in which I was hard pressed to find a vowel. He gave me a phonetic pronunciation, which I wrote down and practiced many times before his introduction. There was an audible intake of breath from the audience when I whipped out the panelist's name without stumbling; they hadn't had a clue about how to pronounce it either. As a moderator, it's impolite and unprofessional to introduce some panelists and then ask the others to bail you out by pronouncing their own names. If you can pronounce Smith, you can learn to pronounce the other names as well.

Watch the group in action to help you determine the seating arrangement. When some members of the panel are good friends, try to separate them so they're playing to the audience instead of to each other. Does anyone appear to be shy or inordinately nervous? Put that person next to you. The farther a person is from the moderator, the more likely it is he'll disappear into the woodwork because you, like everyone else, are paying more attention to those who are more vocal. Moderators generally sit either in the middle of the panel or at one end. How the group interacts informally will guide you in deciding where to position yourself.

Although you may offer refreshments before the panel session, water is the drink of choice both before and during the presentation. An after-dinner panel can be either giggly or contentious if panel members have had a before-dinner drink and a couple glasses of wine with their meal. Alcohol loosens tongues and inhibitions, and even slightly uninhibited panelists may say things they regret later.

When it's time for the presentation, welcome the audience warmly, set out the ground rules for the occasion, and begin your carefully crafted introductions, each one of which should take no more than thirty seconds. Refer to your notes if necessary, but don't read your introductions. You've practiced several times, so you shouldn't need more than one note card per panelist.

It's deadly dull to introduce every panelist in the same way, so keep interest high from the outset by varying the introductions. You might start one with, "Carlos Gonzales is CFO of General Consolidated Manufacturing," but begin another, "Chairwoman of Asian Elegance, LLC, Lucy Nakamura began her career . . ." Another could start with, "Also with us today is John Musical, Director of Marketing at Fiddles and Bows, Limited."

Unless you are both moderator and panel member, which is a tricky combo to pull off, you now take a secondary position. The audience has come to hear the panel, so unless you have something unique to offer, your job is to be alert and keep things moving.

Whether you're a panelist or the moderator, prepare as completely as possible, but don't forget to have a good time. You're on the dais, not the guillotine, so enjoy your interactions with your copanelists and the audience, and savor the advantages of being an expert.

Using a Crib Sheet

Moderating a panel presents several challenges, and there's no reason to work without a net. Unexpected happenings can cause you to forget important facts and details; a single sheet of paper with hints and prompts can make the difference between a panel that limps and one that soars. Here's an example of an effective crib sheet.

> *Title of panel:* Workplace Lawsuits: Protecting Yourself and Your Company
>
> I. *Audience welcome*
>   A. Thank Eleanor for introducing me; now my pleasure to introduce the panel
> II. *Names of panelists*
>   A. Brendan Smith
>   B. Ernestine Bodell (Bo-DELL)
>   C. Clark Johanson (YO-han-son, *not* Jo-HAN-son)
>   D. Ellen Parker
>   E. Frances O'Toole

III. *Seating of panelists (left to right)*
      O'Toole, Bodell, Parker, Smith, Johanson
IV.   *Order of introductions*
      Bodell, Parker, Smith, Johanson, O'Toole
V.   *Introductions*
VI.   *Opening questions*
      A. What are the most common types of workplace lawsuits filed today?
      B. As employees file suit against their employers, is management learning anything?
VII. *Q & A starter questions* (Some of these questions may be planted in the audience so the question-and-answer period is kicked off quickly, and the audience doesn't sit there like looking like an oil painting while someone gets up the nerve to ask a question.)
      A. What's the most difficult aspect of protecting yourself in a lawsuit filed by an employee? (Francine Williams, in audience)
      B. What's the ratio of single-incident suits to class action suits?
      C. Have any verdicts surprised you? Why?
      D. Which types of lawsuits do you think have the most far-reaching effects? (Steve Black, in audience)
VIII. *Closing*
      A. Thanks to panelists (lead applause)
      B. Panel members will be in the Franklin Room during the break for further discussion

MEETING THE MEDIA

In today's world, the need for expert, credible information is unprecedented. There are more channels of communication than ever before, from small community newspapers to twenty-four-hour cable news outlets to millions of Web sites that require continual updating.

The thirst for information is so great that people who might not have been interviewed in the past—midlevel managers, private consultants, CPAs from smaller firms, even massage therapists and dentists—end up in the pages of the newspaper or being quoted on Web sites. Almost anyone is fodder for some type of reportage, and it's good to be ready in case opportunity knocks.

You might receive requests for interviews because your company is in the news and the news is good. Or, your company's in the news and the news is bad. Equally likely is that the company hasn't been in the news at all, and someone from corporate communication has made overtures to the media for coverage. You may be interviewed by print journalists or television and radio reporters or any combination, depending on the immediacy and importance of your story.

If you're looking for a way to stand out, a media interview may be the perfect opportunity—if you're prepared and conduct yourself professionally. How you handle the media may catapult you to stardom in your company.

WHO'S IN CHARGE? THE SURPRISING ANSWER

A media interview is an interchange—an active, participatory process in which you and the reporter have specific roles. Although it may appear that the reporter holds all the cards and you are in the reactive position, the fact is that neither one of you has the upper hand. Without sources, there's no story, so you're as important a part of the equation as the journalist.

Don't get too puffed up by the idea of being a celebrity. Those who think they're doing the media a favor by being available are usually the same people who believe they can wing an interview. Not so. Being unprepared is a sure way to hurt yourself.

If you don't have time to be interviewed, you can always decline, but if you have a few hours or even a day or so to do some background work, you can garner impressive rewards.

Representing your company in a positive way increases the company's visibility and positions you to be noticed both inside your own company and by those who might become interested in stealing you away. Once you've agreed to the interview:

Obtain copies of the publication, read the Web site, or watch or listen to the program for which you'll be interviewed. What kinds of stories does the reporter write? What is the slant of the publication? Does it appear to push a specific point of view? Is it a liberal or conservative show? Does the program's agenda jibe with your own beliefs, or is it likely you'll be treated as an adversary? Is the interviewer folksy or confrontational? Are you prepared for both styles? What's the size of the audience, and is it an audience that's important to your business? If you're on television or radio, will you be part of a panel of experts or the only guest?

Find out all you can about the interviewer. Most television and some newspaper Web sites have navigation buttons that lead to biographies of the reporters. You can determine whether your interviewer is a novice or a seasoned journalist, a specialist or a generalist, and if he's won any awards for investigative or feature reporting.

Ask questions. What is the gist or angle of the interview? Are there specific points the reporter will want you to cover? How long will the interview take?

Write your own questions. Once you know the slant of the story, create the questions you think the interviewer may ask. Have others contribute suggestions to your question bank. Media-savvy coworkers and friends may think of some you haven't considered.

Create concise answers to your questions. Find out early in your preparation if you are the single source for the story or one of many. The greater the number of sources, the more important balance becomes. In a typical multisource print story for a newspaper, you, along with others, may be quoted only once. If you're among many sources for a TV or a radio story, your answer may be edited to less than eight seconds.

Quick Tip: Don't Be a Loose Cannon

If you work for a company that has a corporate communications department and the request for an interview wasn't funneled through that office, ask the reporter if you can get back with her in a few minutes. Place an immediate call to the media relations person in your company and tell him you've been approached. Some companies have very strict guidelines about who speaks to the media, and talking out of turn can get you into hot water. Most reporters know and respect the protocols regarding corporate interviews, but someone who's received a tip may try an end run. Refuse to be intimidated; say nothing until you've been cleared to do so.

In addition, if you see reporters and camera operators in your facility and no one appears to be accompanying them, call corporate communications right away. Reporters have a right to be in any part of the building where the public is allowed, but someone from your company should know they're in the house.

It's critical to your success that your responses be succinct, quotable, and not easily cut.

Practice. Find a friend, family member, or coworker to act the part of the reporter. Give him your prepared questions, but also allow your practice partner some leeway in interviewing you. Good reporters listen carefully and often ask additional questions suggested by your previous responses. Your partner should do that, too. You don't want to be caught off guard by a question you haven't even considered.

Have your colleague critique not only your answers themselves but also your consistency, focus, and style. Did you allow yourself to be sidetracked and diverted, or did you stay on message? Did you avoid vocalized pauses? Did you maintain eye contact and appear professional and at ease? All of these things are important adjuncts to the oral presentation.

The Importance of Message

Without a doubt, the most important thing you can do to prepare for an interview is to decide on the key messages you
want to get across to those who are reading the interview or
listening to what you have to say. You've agreed to the interview because you have a few specific points, usually three to
five, you want to make. Every question a reporter asks you is
an opportunity to feature one of these key points, and if the
reporter asks an off-message question, you can use a phrase
that builds a bridge between the question and the message you
want to accentuate. "The real question here is . . . ," "Let's
look at this issue in context," and "Let me amplify your question a little bit" are examples of bridges that you can use to get
back on message.

Never use these "bridging" techniques to *avoid* answering
questions. Use bridges to swing the reporter's attention to your
preferred topic. The more you stick to your subject, the more
successful your interview will be. You can use a bridge immediately after the question is asked to take you quickly to your message, or you can give a brief answer and then use the bridge to
augment your initial statement. Take a look at these examples:

Question: "Mr. Bailey, do you know what closing your
local operations will mean to the economy
of this town?"

Bridge: "I think you're really asking if we have any
policies in place that will lessen the economic impact of the plant closure. We do."

Message: "Here are some things we've already implemented to make things easier. Every
employee who requests retraining for any
kind of job will have it. Our severance
package is one of the most liberal in the
country. We're giving every employee six

months' full salary; employees also keep their full health benefits for the same period. We've been working hard with other local companies to see if we can place any of our employees with them. They're been very cooperative and helpful, and we've identified fifty comparable positions already. And if employees want to stay with the company in one of our other locations, they'll get first crack at new postings for which they're qualified—and we'll offer relocation assistance."

Question: "You didn't answer my question. Every local business will suffer when you pull out. What are the businesses that depend on yours supposed to do?"

Answer: "You're right. Businesses are interdependent . . ."

Bridge: ". . . and our transition plans indicate we've given the matter a great deal of thought."

Message: "Because we're ensuring six months' full salary, people will still have the money they need to buy the goods and services that keep the local economy moving. Our job retraining program and local job match will help people stay in the community so the economy won't take as big a hit as it otherwise might. We can't guarantee there will be no effects, but we're actively involved in mitigating them. This has been our community for many years, too, and we care about the people here."

Question: "One more question. Why was this decision announced with no warning?"

Bridge: "That's a surprising question because from our viewpoint, this is not a sudden announcement."

Answer: "We've been very open with the media throughout our tenure here. You've been covering our difficulties with this division for more than a year, and you know we've been struggling with rapidly rising costs and directly competing foreign products that are much less expensive. You've reported that our stopgap measures were unsuccessful. The closure was the worst case, and unfortunately, it's come to pass."

Message: "It is unfortunate, but I'm proud of the actions we're taking to lessen the impact for our employees and the community. Job retraining, guaranteed salaries for a significant period of time, a local job match, and opportunities to transfer within the company all reflect our mission of putting our employees first."

The Care and Feeding of Reporters

Reporters are usually nice people who demand respect for only two things: deadlines and the truth. No matter what the medium, journalists are always working on a deadline. When you receive a call, respond as quickly as possible, inquire about the deadline, and do all you can to accommodate it. That doesn't mean you must grant an immediate interview. Ask for a few minutes to gather the facts you need. Then call the reporter back either to do the interview on the phone or to arrange a face-to-face meeting. Start preparing for that meeting immediately.

Keep in mind that if you make yourself scarce or don't respond by the deadline, it doesn't kill the story. The reporter will just move on to another source. Since the story will be written or produced with or without you, it's probably in your best interest to take advantage of the opportunity to contribute.

If you perform well, management probably will look kindly on it. Moreover, you're gaining experience that could bring you to the attention of other potential employers, should you decide to seek a position with another company. A video or a clutch of articles that convey your ability to speak well gives you an advantage other candidates may not have.

Never lie to reporters during an interview or at any other time. Keep the respect of journalists by keeping your word. If you say you'll call a reporter with information before his deadline, make the call; if you're too busy, delegate the task to someone else. When you're being interviewed, you're not obligated to tell everything you know, but what you choose to say must be the truth. As in other situations, a lie will always be uncovered eventually, and your credibility may be irreparably damaged. In fact, lying to a reporter may be a mistake that ends your career.

General Hints and Techniques

When you're interviewing with any journalist, print or electronic, make sure to follow these rules:

Get your key points on the table as quickly as you can, and have your supporting facts, details, and illustrations available for backup. However, don't recite lists of statistics or dry data; use background information only to create clear, pertinent sound bites.

Speak simply. This is not the time to trot out a string of buzzwords or jargon the majority of people can't decipher. I recently witnessed a painful television interview with a well-known attorney who had just won a high-profile case. The interview lasted nearly an hour, and the lawyer used the phrase *at the end of the day* at least once in every answer. It became so annoying I couldn't continue listening to him.

Be friendly and open, not guarded and argumentative. No matter what happens or how aggressive the questions become, remain calm and dignified. Remember that you have control of your message; no one can make you say anything you don't choose to say.

Assume that any remark you make before, during, or after the interview is on the record. Assume that every camera is rolling and every microphone is open. From the time you greet the reporter until you wave good-bye, don't say anything you don't want to see in the story. Watch your language, too. Expletives have no place in interviews.

Insist on accuracy. If the reporter's facts are wrong, correct her. You don't have to jump down her throat; a restatement is enough. "Wendy, I'm afraid that figure is inaccurate. Three percent of our customers reported a defect in the software, not thirty percent."

Don't ask to see the story before it's printed or aired. The reporter may allow you to check facts, but what you said was what you said, and you don't get the opportunity to rewrite it or edit the tape. You may not always be satisfied with the result, but keep it in perspective.

A friend of mine recently answered a reporter's question by saying, "I've never really thought about it precisely that way before, but . . ." In the paper, she was quoted as saying, "I've never really thought about it." She believed the quote made her sound foolish and unprofessional, and she was miffed. However, within the context of the total story, it wasn't that damaging. Be prepared for the fact that your words will be edited; make your message as tight as you can.

Say thank you. Unless the story was an out-and-out hatchet job, send a note of appreciation to the reporter for his efforts.

Take up any concerns with the reporter first. If you're unhappy with the substance of a story, give the reporter a chance to answer your questions about what went wrong. Don't go over his head to the editor or news director. For example, if you hated the headline, the reporter probably didn't write it, and if the story was hacked to pieces, the editor probably chopped it to make it fit the inches available for it. There's a chain of command in newsrooms just as there is in any other business, and you're wise to try to work things out at the lowest level.

Acing the Print Interview

Print interviews may last longer than their radio and television counterparts. Although most print reporters are on daily deadlines for tomorrow's paper, some stories or a series of articles may take weeks or even months to complete. Because they sometimes have the luxury of a little more time to develop a story, print reporters might ask you to expand your answers, so be ready to provide more background information than you might for other types of interviews.

If you're intimidated by the cameras and equipment that are part of the television interview, you'll probably feel much more relaxed chatting with a print journalist in person or on the phone. No matter how comfortable or important the reporter makes you feel, though, never forget you're being interviewed. It's conversation with a purpose. Keep the interview on track by reiterating and amplifying your messages from the beginning to the end.

Don't let the intimacy of a face-to-face interview lead you to confide things you normally wouldn't, even if you say you want to go off the record. Off the record sometimes doesn't work. Suppose you tell a reporter something juicy off the record, and another source tells her exactly the same thing on the record. Or, in following up your tidbit, she uncovers documents that substantiate what you told her. Suppose also that the information she's discovered is critical to the story.

You've now placed the reporter on the horns of a dilemma. If she doesn't report what she's found out, the story is incomplete. If she does, you'll never trust her again, and you can damage her reputation by putting out the word that she's unethical, even though she did nothing wrong. Make it easier for both of you by staying on the record all the time.

A former investigative journalist I know well says,

> "Off the record" really shouldn't come up at all. Better to say "not for attribution." That means I can report what you said; I just can't say I got it from you. If I learn something that's important to a story and it's off the record, you can bet your bottom dollar I'll find some other way to confirm it, and then I can use it—and I will.

Beware of silences. Journalists like to pause just to see if you'll add anything, and sometimes those pauses can be lengthy. Rushing to fill the silence gives you more opportunities to trip yourself up. If you've finished your answer, stop talking and wait quietly for the next question.

Working the Electronic Room

Television offers several ways of being interviewed. The reporter may come to you, or you may go to the station to be interviewed on set or as part of a panel or talk show. In-the-field interviews go by very quickly, and you must be ready to make your key points immediately. Don't waste valuable air time; keep your answers as short and compelling as you can make them.

An on-set interview is also a hit-and-run opportunity. Most segments are very brief, offering you no more than three, and possibly fewer, chances to answer questions. Laserlike focus on your most important message is essential to make the most of these occasions.

Panels or point-counterpoint appearances can be more problematic than interviews in which you're the only subject. Ask who's sharing the screen with you so you can be ready for the types of arguments you might encounter. Prepare very thoroughly and have all the facts and data you need right at the tip of your brain. These fast-paced programs can make you uncomfortable if others, especially those in the opposite camp, are better able to present their case. Keep your messages succinct and illustrate them with simple, easy-to-remember examples. That's what the other side will do.

No matter what, keep a firm grip on your temper. No screaming, no yelling, no belittling—be courteous. Once a question is asked, you must move into the arena quickly so you don't lose your chance to speak, but once you have the floor, maintain your composure and make your points professionally. You can be very assertive and forceful without being insolent and contemptuous, by using any of these examples:

- "There's nothing you've said that I can agree with."
- "I disagree completely."
- "We differ on almost every point."
- "Although I agree that this is a serious problem, my solution is very different from the one you're proposing."

Avoid such attacks as these:

- "How can you possibly believe that what you're proposing makes any sense?"
- "That's idiotic."
- "Clearly, you haven't thought your ideas through, or you'd see they don't work."

The idea is to refute the opponent's idea, not savage the opponent himself. However, if your counterpart is not as polite as you are and interrupts you at every turn, you might say something like one of the following statements:

- "John, I'd appreciate the opportunity to finish my answer."
- "John, I'd prefer not to interrupt you, but I can't find another way to make myself heard."

- "John, I have some more time remaining. I'll give you the floor when my time is up."
- "John, please stop interrupting me. I'll show you the same courtesy when it's your turn."
- "John, this is supposed to be an exchange, not a monologue, and I'm going to go on even if you persist in interrupting me."

These statements are all well within the boundaries of polite discourse. However, if your counterpart absolutely refuses to let you speak, you can always appeal to the moderator. Doing so makes you look as if you can't defend yourself, however, so try to hold your ground with civility.

If you're volatile and easily baited, you may not be the best person to speak. There's no rule that says you have to participate, so if you have a colleague who's knowledgeable and more even-tempered than you are, it might be smart to pass this event along. A bad showing could have a negative effect on your standing within your company, and you must remember that when you're in the public eye, you represent not only yourself, but also your boss, your coworkers, and even the CEO. Any display of temper or arrogance on your part makes them look bad, too.

Whatever type of television interview you're doing, look at the host or other participants, not at the camera. Cameras may move during your interview, and while you're twisting around trying to locate them, you're not zeroing in on your messages. Just converse with the person who's interviewing you, and let the camera operator worry about finding you.

Don't forget, however, that the reporter is your gateway to the audience you want to reach. Although your eyes are trained on her, your carefully crafted messages are designed for them. Stick with what you came to say.

Because television is a visual medium, your words are underscored by the way you deliver them. Make your body language congruent with what you say. Sit forward a bit; look as if you're having a good time. Television magnifies gestures, so

don't wave your arms around, even if you're usually an ani-
mated speaker. Sometimes you'll be seated in a swivel chair.
Whatever you do, resist the urge to twirl or rock the chair. You'll
look nervous and all that motion will make viewers seasick.

On camera, stripes may bleed and checks strobe, so it's
best to choose neutral, solid-colored clothing without much
design. You want your audience to pay attention to your
words, not to the dazzling effects created by your wardrobe. If
you expect to be interviewed often, it's wise to keep "interview
clothes" in your office so you can change your jacket or shirt
if necessary.

There's a famous scene in the movie *Broadcast News* in
which the empty-headed anchorman tells the seasoned journalist how to look good on camera. "Sit on your coat," he says,
and you know what? It's good advice. If you're wearing a suit
jacket or sport coat, tucking the bottom of your jacket under
your derriere gives a smoother fit; it keeps the shoulders from
bunching up and the neck from gapping.

Check your appearance just before you go on. Straighten
your tie, tame your hair, breathe, relax, and enjoy your on-
camera moment.

Talking without Pictures

Radio is the most intimate medium of them all. People watching television may have many others around them: family,
coworkers, even strangers on adjacent bar stools. On the other
hand, radio listeners are often alone in their cars, cubicles,
kitchens, or even in the shower, so you're speaking to many
audiences of one. The host stands in for these individual audiences; you converse with him as their surrogate. Let your personality, warmth, and excitement about your subject come
through, just as they would if you were speaking with a close
friend. Smile when it's appropriate; it's surprising how audible
a pleasant facial expression can be.

Radio and print interviews often are conducted on the
phone, which means you can keep your key messages right in

front of you and refer to them as often as you wish. That's a huge plus that's not available to you on television. Notes are helpful whether the interview is a fifteen-second sound bite or a wide-ranging, long-format conversation. Naturally, you don't read your notes over the phone; you use them only as reminders to ensure that you cover all your important points.

When doing a remote phone interview, whether for radio or print, call from a corded phone, rather than a cell or cordless phone or headset. Batteries have a way of giving up the ghost at the wrong minute, and cell calls can fade or drop out altogether. Turn off call waiting; beeping in the middle of an interview is unprofessional—and for heaven's sake, if you've forgotten to disable call waiting, don't compound the error by taking the call!

It's very important to find out—and then confirm—how long your interview will be. I once was told I'd be on the air for ten minutes. An hour later, I emerged from the broadcast booth bathed in sweat because I'd made all my best points within the first eight minutes, and the reporter couldn't seem to come up with any questions beyond those I'd written for her. She and I were both neophytes at the interview game, and neither of us quite knew what to do. We back-filled and repeated ourselves and sounded clumsy and inept. Recalling that interview still makes me blush, and the memory probably doesn't bring a smile to her face, either. Today, I'd come armed with an extensive list of backup questions, examples, stories, and surprising facts.

Talk radio hosts run the gamut from ghastly to great. Some are prepared; some haven't done any background work at all. Some ask a question and back off; others are in your face before you've finished a sentence, interrupting and badgering. Some use the microphone to showcase their own brilliance, while others are generous about letting you shine.

Call-in shows are challenging but interesting. Your job is to answer the questions; the host manages the guests. She cuts off those who ramble, clarifies questions, and keeps things humming. Although you never know what's going to come out of a caller's mouth, that's part of the excitement, so go with the flow. You may learn as much from the callers as they do from you, and lively interchanges keep you from dozing over the microphone. Show respect for every caller and every question, stick close to your messages, and you'll have a good time.

> ### Quick Tip: See You Later
>
> You, not the television station, are responsible for arranging to have your television interview videotaped. If you forget to have a colleague or family member do the honors, there are services that videotape local news broadcasts, and they'll edit and sell you what you need. These tapes are invaluable aids for improving your on-air performance and for selling yourself for future jobs.

Answering the Tough Questions

Reporters sometimes resort to very aggressive questioning techniques, especially if they think you're withholding something or aren't telling the whole truth. (And, incidentally, people within your own organization who want to diminish your star power may very well use the same kinds of techniques against you in meetings. Learning how to deal with these problematic issues may serve you in the boardroom as well as in the media.) Here are some styles of questions to look out for:

Either A or B. "Are you laying people off because you've made the decision to send the jobs out of the country or because the company is in trouble?" In this type of question, neither alternative may be true. The real answer may very well be C, so don't fall into the forced-choice trap.

Disregard the alternatives and deliver your own message: "We expect these layoffs to be temporary. A slump in sales has resulted in an increase in inventory. We are taking steps to remedy that situation, and we hope to call our people back within three months."

The speculative question. "If the economy doesn't turn

around, will you make the layoffs permanent?" Don't be pushed into a corner and talk about what might happen.

No one knows what the future holds; stick with the here and now: "I really don't like to respond to what-ifs. We fully expect that our attempts to turn this temporary situation around will be successful. The steps we're taking include . . ."

The unattributed source. "There are rumors that these layoffs are just the tip of the iceberg because the company is going under."

Don't give credence to people the reporter doesn't name. Deflect the issue and repeat your message: "I think it's best to stick to the facts, and the fact is that these layoffs are a temporary measure."

See all that bridging? Three questions, and three times the reporter has learned that the layoffs are temporary. That's good preparation and tenacious focus on the message.

The One Thing Not to Say

There may be times that you legitimately cannot answer a question. Perhaps there's a lawsuit pending, or it's early in a

---

Quick Tip: The Loaded Question

Never repeat a loaded or defamatory question. If a reporter asks it, it's just a question that won't go into the story, but the minute *you* say it, you've put it on the record and your total answer can be quoted. "No, I've never starred in a porno movie," may come out as part of a headline: "Family Values Cookies' CEO Denies Porn Industry Past." Equally bad, it may be used as the tease for television news: "What local executive says she's never been a porn star? The answer will surprise you—find out at eleven." Guess who wins the ratings race that night? And, of course, it's uploaded to the Internet and beamed around the world almost before you've finished your denial. Don't give the question a starring role in your answer.

crisis and all the facts aren't in. The question may be tasteless and crude. No matter what the reason for not answering, never say "no comment." A heads-up journalist will seize on it, wonder what you're concealing, and pester you until he gets some kind of response. "No comment" makes you look as guilty as the mob boss being led away in handcuffs with his coat over his head. In addition, the reporter can legitimately claim that you refused to answer the question.

When you can't respond to a question, come out from behind "no comment" and be as truthful, forthcoming, and candid as the circumstances will allow. Make good on any promise to help the reporter develop the story:

- "I can't comment on that question, because I don't know the answer. I'll make some calls and get back to you no later than two hours from now."
- "Here is a statement from the general counsel's office. Because litigation is involved, I can't expand on it."
- "You're asking me to speculate and I won't do that. When I have facts, I'll tell you."
- "Your question is insulting to my family, and I have no intention of answering it."

Members of the media can be of immense value to your organization, especially at times of confusion and uncertainty, but if you have lied, distorted the truth, or given them any other reason to distrust you, don't expect reporters to rush to your aid when you need them. Play fast and loose with media representatives at your own risk.

Public appearances, live or through media channels, can help you make your move to the top. They can demonstrate your ability to think quickly, respond appropriately, and maintain your poise. They showcase your professionalism and your competence in communicating. Management values every one of these attributes and frequently rewards them with promotions and pay increases. So get out there and show your stuff. If your current company doesn't appreciate your efforts, your next one probably will.

Be a public star:

- Develop the communications skills that make you comfortable in any public setting
- Take every opportunity to showcase yourself and your company
- Keep your company's key messages in the forefront whenever you speak
- Stay positive, even in negative situations
- Listen at least as much as you talk

PART THREE

TYING IT UP

11

SOUNDING SMART
WHEREVER YOU ARE

ON THE ROAD: WORKING THE TRADE SHOW

Trade shows are big business all over the world, and it's a compliment to be asked to represent your company at a booth. It's also a trust: you are being trusted to behave professionally and to epitomize the substance and style of your company. It's a big responsibility, but unfortunately, many trade show representatives don't take advantage of the opportunity to showcase themselves as well as their employers. They treat the event as a chore and those who visit the booth as annoyances, and that's not the way to generate enthusiasm about a product or service.

Although sales are sometimes made at trade shows, the real purpose of going on the road to spotlight your products is to find potential customers and qualify them for later sales efforts. As a booth worker, you are the first point of contact for your company. You can lead a prospect down the path toward being a customer, or you can turn her off in the first fifteen seconds. To be effective at trade shows:

Have a goal. Perhaps you want to qualify twenty prospects a day or ensure that no one leaves your booth without company literature. A goal helps keep you focused when the crowd dwindles or the day seems long.

Dress the part. If they are not formally dressed, trade show representatives often wear an event uniform. If you're wearing such an outfit, informality is acceptable—but sloppiness isn't. Your clothes should be clean and neatly pressed. Men should shave or groom their facial hair; women's makeup should be natural, not garish. Fingernails must be clean and well manicured. Because you'll be on your feet for a long time, wear attractive but very comfortable shoes. There's no excuse for going barefoot when meeting potential customers.

Furthermore, if you've been partying with industry colleagues, make sure you avail yourself of mouthwash, eyedrops, and anything else you need to appear prepared and on top of your game.

Act happy to be there. Nothing is less attractive to a potential client than a salesperson who looks bored, disengaged, or indifferent. Keep a smile on your face and be ready to greet whoever comes to your booth. You cannot be ready if you're eating or drinking, so save those activities for your breaks. Most places don't allow smoking in the booth, but even if your venue permits it, don't light up. The smell and threat of secondhand smoke will cause some customers to pass you by. Consider the front of your booth the door to your office, and meet the client as if he were coming to see you there. Be relaxed, confident, and welcoming.

Spend time with customers, not with fellow booth workers. If you're engaged in a spirited conversation with your coworkers and have your back to the sales floor, very few people are going to try to break through. Qualified prospects rush by as they look for a friendlier environment.

Stand up, introduce yourself, shake hands, make eye contact, and qualify prospects with open-ended questions. Questions that require nothing more than a yes or no answer stop conversation cold; open-ended questions keep the lines of communication humming. Here are some to consider:

- "Good morning [if the prospect is wearing a name tag, use his name], Mr. Gotbucks. I'm Bonnie Schwartz. I see you're from California; we do a lot of business there. What brings you to the show this year?"
- "What products are you currently using? How are they working for you?"
- "What features would make your lift truck [storm door, corporate jet] better?"
- "What goes into your decision-making process when you buy a product like ours?" (If he can't tell you, you're talking to the wrong person. Nonetheless, don't drop your current prospect with a thud. He may have considerable influence with the decision maker. Try to find out if the decision maker is present and invite the prospect to return with that person. If there's no hope of meeting the decision maker, continue speaking pleasantly with the booth visitor, but disengage after a few more minutes. You need to spend your time with those who can actually buy your products.)
- "I'd like to have someone follow up with you after the show. When would be the best time for us to get back in touch with you?"

As always, the most important part of asking a question is listening to the answer. Few things are more annoying to a customer than a canned hard sell that makes no allowance for individual differences. Concentrate on the customer's unique needs and how your product or service can solve his problems.

Hand sales literature to the prospect personally. Most trade show booths contain piles of slicks and brochures to be scooped up by anyone who passes by. Many people collect this literature as a first step in qualifying a company to do business with. However, keep your expensive sales pieces out of sight and reserve them for qualified leads; make sure these people understand that the literature is reserved for special people: "Mr. Gotbucks, I'd like you to have a more detailed explanation of our products, so here's a packet we give out only when we think there's a real fit between what you need and what we can provide. It should answer many of your questions, and I'll be following up if you need more information or explanation. Thanks so much for coming to talk with us today. We appreciate your taking the time to ask us about what we can do for you."

Last, watch your words. An informal atmosphere doesn't give you license to pepper your speech with profanity, inappropriate humor, or substandard English. Your booth is a business location, and you must behave there as you would behave in the home office.

If your time on the road brings in qualified prospects, you buff your reputation as a great company representative and improve your chances for advancement.

ON THE ROAD: SMALL WORLD, ISN'T IT?

Business is business, and though you should be friendly, approachable, and courteous to everyone, you must watch what you say not only in your hometown but also when you're away with your colleagues or others in your industry. Never believe that the remarks you make away from the office won't find their way back. Most industry groups—from software engineers to corporate pilots to event planners—are relatively small communities, and what people say has a way of getting around. You must choose your words carefully no matter where you are.

For example, say you're at a trade show talking to a counterpart in the next booth. He says, "What do you think of your new VP of sales?"

"Well," you reply, "just between us, she's a gigantic pain—demanding, nasty, a witch with her very own broom."

And he says, "Really? She's always been my favorite aunt." In one sentence, you've knifed your career in the heart. There's no way you can back out of your statement, switch nametags with a coworker, or disappear through a hole in the floor.

And if you think the nephew won't tell his aunt, then you

live in some other universe. Update your résumé now; you're going to need it.

Obviously, this is an extreme example, but ill-considered remarks can haunt you. Some of your colleagues are real friends and would never divulge the source of an inappropriate, thoughtless statement. Others are not so honorable; they'd be happy to step over you on their climb up the corporate hill. In addition, you never know who's overhearing your conversation. Think before you speak, and always avoid:

Publicly criticizing anyone in your company—peers, subordinates, or superiors. Even if you're baited, and even if you agree wholeheartedly with a negative assessment of someone else, keep those feelings to yourself. Focus on the person's good qualities. "Oh, I know people say she's a taskmaster, but she works herself as hard as she works everyone else." Or, "I think he just wants exceptional performance from everyone and gets frustrated sometimes." You can always vent your feelings at home, but make office communication positive. You can't be taken to task for something you didn't say.

Discussing a coworker's personal attributes. I once hired a man who happened to be extraordinarily attractive. I added him to my staff because of his skills, experience, and work ethic, but it was impossible not to notice that he was also a very handsome fellow. I happened to comment on that one day to a colleague. Two weeks later, my assistant told me it was all around the building that I said I'd hired Craig for his looks. That was a disservice to me, of course, but especially to him, because he was an effective leader and hard worker. I learned two lessons that day: one was not to mention physical features; the second was never to trust my colleague again.

There was a third thing I found out, too: my assistant had my back. That was good for me and better for her. Her bravery in informing me of what was being said about me caused me to appreciate, value, and trust her. Because she had earned my trust, I mentored her, encouraging her to take more responsibility and live up to her potential. She now has more college degrees than I do and a job with far more responsibility than being someone else's assistant.

Breaking a confidence. A confidence is sacred. Your word must be your bond. Colleagues may conclude that if you'd break a personal confidence, you might also share business information or trade secrets with those outside the company. Trust is imperative in business, and once you've broken faith with your associates, your chances for advancement dwindle.

Spreading gossip and rumors. For many people, gossip is fun. If you have something juicy to share, you feel powerful. For a moment you get to sit at the table with the "cool kids." You're a member of the in crowd. But gossip is almost always at someone else's expense, and it generally involves something negative, or it wouldn't be such a desirable tidbit.

Rumors are items that have been repeated often enough to give them staying power and a ring of truth. But the appearance of truth is not the same as truth. If you'd like a dramatic example of rumors that have worked their away around the world on the Internet, go to www.snopes.com; there are hundreds on the site, and very few of them contain even a scintilla of truth.

Passing along gossip and rumors can be dangerous. If your information is later found to be inaccurate, you can look careless, naive, and mean spirited, and no manager wants to promote an associate who doesn't have the sense to investigate the difference between fact and fiction—and who is nasty as well. A second danger is more personal: those you gossip about will cut you off, and you'll likely lose valuable channels of important workplace information.

The person who gossiped that I'd hired my associate for his looks enjoyed a moment of seeming in the know. What he forgot was that gossip, true or untrue, gets around, and it often makes its way to the person who is its subject. He probably was unaware why we never had a private conversation again. Although I refrained from trying to hurt him professionally, I never went out of my way to help him, either.

Gossip also wastes valuable time. Those who are gossiping aren't working, and that's cheating those who write your paycheck. Be smart by refusing to participate in gossip. You needn't be condescending and superior; you simply say, "I'm not comfortable talking about this. I have lots to do and I need to get back to work."

For a while, others may view you as a stick-in-the-mud, but it's also possible your attitude may inspire others to tone down the gossip. If that happens, the workplace will be a more productive and pleasant environment for everyone. People will be free to work without worrying about what others are saying about them. You'll be in a position of leadership because people know they can trust you; they're much more likely to share relevant information, and it's good information, not rumors and innuendo, that gives you the power to advance.

Greek philosopher Epictetus said, "We have two ears and one mouth so we can listen twice as much as we speak." He was on to something.

Speaking under the influence of alcohol. When you're away from the office in the convivial setting of a trade show or a training session, it's sometimes relaxing to have a drink and some conversation with colleagues. But drinking far into the evening can make you sloppy and obnoxious. You may say things that are highly offensive and perhaps even actionable. You might not remember them the next morning, but your coworkers will. And if you've been unlucky enough to demonstrate such poor judgment in front of those from other companies in your industry, you're not going to be the person they try to steal away with offers of promotion and a big salary.

Giving away proprietary information. You might never think of divulging company secrets when you're in the vicinity of your workplace, but when you're just shooting the breeze in a banquet line at an industry event, it's easy to let something slip. The other person mentions that his company is adding a new product, and you pipe up, "Yeah, we heard about that, and we're going to beat you to the punch. We're already in production."

It's hard to overstate the damage you've just done to your career path with your current employer. When you're privy to confidential information, nothing short of torture should cause you to talk about it. At best, it can be career ending, and if you share insider financial information with family and friends and they act on it and profit from it, you can end up behind bars for longer than you'd like to consider.

Talking too freely about wanting to leave your current employer. Maybe your work situation is intolerable. You can't stand your boss; your colleagues are insufferable, and the work is stultifying. You want out. While you're at a cocktail party, an executive from another company approaches you and starts to chat about work. She mentions that she'll soon have an opening. Do you know anyone who might be interested?

What you say next is important. If you blurt out, "Please, consider me. I'm dying to leave! You know Stan. He's impossible, and Gene's no better. I know I could do a great job for you," don't be surprised if the executive suddenly melts into the crowd, rather like the baseball players who disappear into the corn in the movie *Field of Dreams.* Your statements have been disloyal and unprofessional—and possibly overheard. You've been less than smart.

A far better response is, "Let me think about it. Let's exchange business cards, and I'll call you when I get back to the city."

When you return home, you can call the executive and indi-

Quick Tip: Looking Good on the Road

Being out of town doesn't relieve you of the responsibility of looking like a professional. If there's an industry dinner, award show, or recognition event at a meeting you're attending, dress appropriately. No navel-baring midriff tops for the women, and no lounge singer outfits for the men. You don't have to look as if you're a cloistered nun or monk, but your clothes should be conservative. You want those you meet to remember *you*, not your flashy, unsuitable get-ups. Looking like a scamp or a tramp may make an impression, but it's the wrong one.

cate that you've thought things over and might like to consider the position yourself. If the executive welcomes that idea, you're free to begin a formal interview process that might result in your moving on and up. And you've done it professionally and without burning bridges with your current colleagues.

AN ELEGANT STRATEGY

The essence of every type of communication is consideration for others. Although I'm not a member of Rotary International, I've always admired their statement of business ethics:

Of the things we do, think, or say:
Is it the TRUTH?
Is it FAIR to all concerned?
Will it build GOODWILL and BETTER FRIEND-SHIPS?
Will it be BENEFICIAL to all concerned?

And when it comes to communication, I'd add, is it KIND and is it COURTEOUS? Because courtesy is such a rare commodity today, being polite and putting others' needs on an equal footing with your own can ameliorate many touchy situations, both in and out of the office.

Almost any message goes down better if it's delivered gently and courteously. Instant communication has its advantages, of course, but too often gentility and grace are sacrificed on the altar of speed. Slow it down a little, leaven your speech with some pleasant words and phrases, and you may be amazed at how much more willing people are to listen to you and to act on what you say. Here are some of those important phrases:

Good morning	I'm sorry
Please	I was wrong
Thank you	I'm proud of you
You're welcome	How may I help you?

It's nice to see you

You did a great job

I appreciate your help

What a nice thing to do

I enjoyed working with you

It's a pleasure to meet you

If the stresses of life have removed these sentences from your vocabulary, take them out of mothballs. You'll be glad you did, and so will everyone around you.

Be an everyday star:

- Consider the effect of what you say, both on your company and on your future
- Remember that every setting is a business setting
- Be discreet and maintain confidences
- Use kind words even in tough situations
- Listen as least as much as you talk

12

THE TOP

HOW LEADERS SPEAK

M any aspire to leadership. Most don't make it: some because they don't have the intellect or the drive or the emotional intelligence to read people and situations; others, who may have all the other traits of leadership, because they haven't learned how to communicate, especially when they speak.

Those who depend on overblown business rhetoric and the insulating, isolating gobbledygook that passes for workplace communication today usually are found jockeying for position in the ranks of middle management—if they're lucky—and unless they learn the lessons of those who've reached the top of the business heap, they may never make it out of their current niche. The type of language they use suggests that they have nothing original to say and must rely on flavor-of-the-month verbiage to speak at all.

Although the roster of qualities that constitute the leader's portfolio includes vision, values, skills, character, knowledge, confidence, integrity, and commitment, among others, the sine qua non of true leadership in every sphere of influence is the ability to communicate across a broad range of audiences. The American workplace has changed, is changing, and will continue to change. Leadership by fiat is over; today's leaders must be able to motivate teams, mentor talented associates, and see and seize opportunities. They can't do any of that without the ability to speak effectively about the organization's missions and goals and to spark others' enthusiasm for attaining those objectives.

Great leaders rise above the mundane to the inspiring. What inspires people are not facts and data and figures and charts but stories that appeal to both the intellect and the emotions and challenge people to ponder how the stories apply to them and their lives and work. Leaders paint uplifting narratives that enable the listeners to imagine themselves in the story.

Therefore, those who speak daily of "facilitating strategic thinking," "taking performance to the next level," and "seeking comprehensive solutions" to unarticulated problems may succeed in the short term, but they will not energize, they will not excite, they will not inspire, and they will not lead.

Leaders' speech is inclusive, not exclusionary; easy to follow, not convoluted; and understandable, not shrouded in doublespeak and misdirection. Leaders become leaders because they can articulate a vision and communicate it in ways others can grasp. They can reach out to disparate groups, from the executive suite to the machine shop; engage every person through language that's appropriate, real, and memorable; and rally all their listeners around a common theme.

The late Peter Drucker, the father of management science, once said that managers are concerned with doing things right, while leaders are concerned with doing the right things. I would add that leaders also are concerned with saying the right things—and saying them right.

Powerful communication is not a mystery to be solved but a skill to be learned. The first aspect of the skill is choosing the right words for the situation, and that means developing your vocabulary. Early in the 1920s, Johnson O'Connor, an engineer with General Electric, began to study aptitudes, those qualities that lead us to choose certain occupations and excel in them. Of all his discoveries, one stood out. The greatest predictor of success in *every* area and industry wasn't an aptitude at all but an acquired trait: a person's vocabulary. Today, the Johnson O'Connor Research Foundation continues its work in the study of aptitudes and has made substantial contributions to the literature related to vocabulary. In 1990, additional publications validated O'Connor's initial findings regarding the vocabularies of executives and managers.[1]

A well-tended vocabulary makes it possible to appreciate subtlety and to select words with the shades of meaning that match the circumstances. Possessing a rich vocabulary means you no longer have to be held hostage to the bloated, nonsensical chatter of everyday business speech.

Although O'Connor's work indicated that most people's vocabulary growth slowed after the completion of formal education, there's no reason it has to. Hundreds of books, tapes, and programs allow you to study on your own and increase your vocabulary exponentially.

The more extensive your vocabulary, the more effectively you can use words to create the mental pictures that move others to action. Paradoxically, however, the more you learn, the more you see the necessity for using simple words to express big ideas. Whatever words you choose, be sure you're using them correctly before trying them out at work.

Leaders understand that their message must be understandable to every group that they hope to influence; therefore, as they rise through their organizations, they throw off today's buzzwords and learn to use unadorned, clear speech to win over each audience. They use small words to carry big freight. The real business and industry leaders—the originals who shake things up and make things happen—usually speak quite simply.

Bill Gates, the richest and certainly one of the most influential men on the planet, has an interesting style. When inter-

Quick Tip: Building a More Expressive Vocabulary

An agile vocabulary makes you stand out from the pack, whether you're a job seeker or already settled in your career. To enlarge your vocabulary, do these three things:

Read widely and take notes. Choose authors who will challenge you to think; study how they use words. Read humorists, novelists, essayists, and poets. Read voraciously in your own field to learn how leaders use the language of your profession. Highlight words about which you have questions; look them up and commit them to memory. Say them out loud. Write them in sentences. Use them until they have become old friends.

Learn where words come from. A basic understanding of Latin and Greek word roots will help you translate thousands of words. I once was able to teach a three-year-old the meaning of *submarine* by telling him that *sub* always means "under" and *marine* has to do with the sea. "Oh," he said, "then a submarine goes under the sea." If he can learn it, you can learn it, and it's great fun to be able to tease the meaning from a word you've never understood or never used before.

Use reference books. Dictionaries help you pronounce and define, and a thesaurus guides you in choosing among various words that have similar meanings. Although many people swear by Roget's *Thesaurus*, my dog-eared copy of Rodale's *The Synonym Finder* has never let me down, and it's the easiest book in the world to use.

viewed about computer-specific issues, he can sound like the leader of the technogeek pack; his language is loaded with jargon that the technology community understands. However, when he speaks on other topics, such as education or the crisis in world health, his language is direct and unembellished.

In an interview with the late Peter Jennings, Gates was

asked why his foundation was focused on eradicating communicable diseases. He answered, "The U.S. is very oriented towards solving inequity. . . . The great inequity is that we let people die of these diseases. We treat their lives as being worth less than a few hundred dollars because that's what it would take to save them."[2] It's an eloquent statement expressed in terms any listener, from a middle-school student to the CEO of a multinational corporation, can relate to and understand.

In a 2001 interview, Warren Buffett, one of today's preeminent business leaders, said that interest rates "act as gravity behaves in the physical world. . . . The tiniest change in rates changes the value of every financial asset."[3] Contrast that brief, striking explanation with the definition of the same term below:

A rate which is charged or paid for the use of money. An interest rate is often expressed as an annual percentage of the principal. It is calculated by dividing the amount of interest by the amount of principal. Interest rates often change as a result of inflation and Federal Reserve policies. For example, if a lender (such as a bank) charges a customer $90 in a year on a loan of $1000, then the interest rate would be 90/1000 *100% = 9%.[4]

There's nothing wrong with either one of these definitions; each is appropriate for its purpose, but which one makes you want to keep listening? Which one sticks in your mind? Warren Buffett is famous for his easy-to-grasp style and his ability to make concepts real. It's not the entire reason he's a leader, but it's certainly a part of the leadership package.

Rich white men don't have a corner on the market when it comes to leadership speech. What more influential person is there than Oprah Winfrey, who has interested Americans in reading, eating properly, dealing with child molesters, developing their spiritual lives, and sharing their riches? She is always expressive and speaks from the heart; her speech can be colloquial or elegant, depending on the situation. Whatever style she adopts at the moment, what she says is unambiguous and unequivocal.

In the summer of 2004, Barack Obama, now a US senator from Illinois, delivered a keynote address, which came to be known as "the audacity of hope" speech, at the Democratic National Convention. It was an electrifying performance that catapulted Obama onto the international stage in just a few minutes. At slightly more than two thousand words, the speech was part vision and part autobiography, full of stories and arresting images. He spoke of his parents, his children, his life, and his beliefs. He invited those in attendance to join him in his quest to recover American values and unify the people. With the exception of *inalienable*, *possibilities*, and *individualism*, most of the words of the speech contained four syllables or fewer.

Whatever one's politics, it was impossible not to admire the artistry of the performance and to view Obama as a potential national leader. Although he probably would have won the Senate race anyway, his speech sealed the deal, and at no time did he resort to phrases such as "leveraging the nation's living assets" or "making an impactful statement to the American people."

Leaders also understand the power of vision. They know they must create positive visions and engage people's emotions to generate the kind of commitment required to reach important goals. They're aware that people work harder and more willingly in pursuit of ideals that are loftier than achieving operating efficiencies or production quotas, so they put a larger frame around what they want to accomplish. They consistently communicate ideas such as progress, values, unity, family, and possibilities, and they engender emotion, attention, and interest with striking similes, meaningful metaphors, and apt analogies.

Think of the words that have resonated throughout the twentieth century and beyond and what visions they create

- The only thing we have to fear is fear itself.
- A day which will live in infamy
- I have nothing to offer but blood, toil, tears, and sweat.
- Ask not what your country can do for you
- They will not be judged on the color of their skin, but by the content of their character
- *Ich bin ein Berliner.*
- Our long national nightmare is over.
- Mr. Gorbachev, tear down this wall!

Although they may suggest difficulty and even hardship, each of these phrases creates a powerful picture and invites listeners to participate in the vision. Victory over economic devastation. Preparation for a long and costly war. National service. Racial equality. Rebuilding confidence in government. Freedom itself. Huge ideas expressed simply. That's the language of leaders, and if you aspire to leadership, it's the kind of language you should emulate.

Leaders' nonverbal communication matches what they say, creating an integrity of message that's hard to beat. Leaders, though they may be driven, intense people, are often compassionate and courteous. They are usually respectful of others' space and time, look at others while speaking and listening, talk about issues rather than other people, congratulate and thank those who help them achieve their goals, and ask for their listeners' help in accomplishing great objectives. They are optimistic about possibilities and positive about people's abilities to excel.

In short, leaders do more than talk. They communicate. They understand Mark Twain's famous quotation: "The difference between the almost right word and the right word is really a large matter—it's the difference between the lightning bug and the lightning."[5] Leaders deliver the lightning every time. And with work, time, care, and the willingness to be extraordinary, so can you.

NOTES

CHAPTER 5

1. Quoted in "The Cow in the Ditch: How Anne Mulcahy Rescued Xerox," Knowledge@Wharton Web site, http://knowledge.wharton.upenn.edu/index.cfm?fa=viewArticle&id=1318&specialld=41 (accessed December 12, 2005).

2. Howard Bailen, "US Workers' Trust in Management Is Low: Mercer Survey Reveals a Lack of Confidence in Top Executives," http://www.mercerhr.com/summary.jhtml?idContent=1187220 (accessed November 18, 2005).

CHAPTER 7

1. William Poundstone, *How Would You Move Mount Fuji? Microsoft's Cult of the Puzzle: How the World's Smartest Companies Select the Most Creative Thinkers* (Boston: Little, Brown, 2003).

CHAPTER 8

1. Rob O'Regan, "Do People Really Pay Attention during Online Meetings?" http://www.kolabora.com/news/2005/02/02/do_people_really_pay_attention.htm (accessed October 28, 2005).

2. Linda Kreger Silverman, *Upside-Down Brilliance: The Visual Spatial Learner* (Glendale, CO: DeLeon, 2002), p. iv.

3. "'Here's Looking at You' Has New Meaning: Eye Contact Shown to Affect Conversation Patterns, Group Problem-Solving Ability," Queen's University (Canada) press release, ScienceDaily Web site, http://www.sciencedaily.com/releases/2002/11/021122073858.htm (accessed November 12, 2005).

CHAPTER 12

1. R. C. Gershon, *The Vocabulary Scores of Managers*, Technical Report 1990-5 (Chicago: Johnson O'Connor Research Foundation, 1990).

2. "One-on-One with Bill Gates: Microsoft Chairman Talks to Peter Jennings about Innovation, Competition, Goals," http://abcnews.go.com/WNT/story?id=506354&page=4 (accessed December 28, 2005).

3. Quoted in Carol Loomis, "Warren Buffett on the Stock Market," *Fortune*, December 6, 2001; available in abridged form at http://chinese-school.netfirms.com/Warren-Buffett-interview.html (accessed December 14, 2005).

4. "Interest Rate," http://www.investorwords.com/2539/interest_rate.html (accessed December 14, 2005).

5. Mark Twain, letter to George Bainton, October 15, 1888, quoted at http://www.twainquotes.com/Lightning.html (accessed February 10, 2006).

INDEX